KT-157-857

100 Most *Infamous* Criminals

Murder, mayhem and madness

Jo Durden Smith

This edition published in 2023 by Arcturus Publishing Limited
26/27 Bickels Yard, 151–153 Bermondsey Street,
London SE1 3HA

Copyright © Arcturus Holdings Limited

All rights reserved. No part of this publication may be reproduced, stored in a
retrieval system, or transmitted, in any form or by any means, electronic, mechanical,
photocopying, recording or otherwise, without prior written permission in
accordance with the provisions of the Copyright Act 1956 (as amended). Any
person or persons who do any unauthorised act in relation to this publication may be
liable to criminal prosecution and civil claims for damages.

AD008580UK

Printed in the UK

Contents

United Kingdom

Australia

INTERNATIONAL

SADA ABE

WHEN A POLICE inspector walked into a Tokyo inn room on the afternoon of 20 May 1936 to check out the identity of the occupant, he didn't expect to find 31-year-old Sada Abe. And even after she'd announced who she was, he refused to believe her. Then, though, she took out of her bodice a paper parcel and unfolded it – and the evidence was unmistakable. For it contained the severed genitals of her dead lover, Kichizo Ishida.

The naked body of restaurant-owner Ishida had been found by a chambermaid two days before in a room in the equivalent of a modern love-hotel. Carved onto his thigh and written in blood on a bedsheet were the characters *Sada, Kichi Futari-kiri* (*Sada and Kichi, inseparable forever*). The word Sada had been written on his left arm. His penis and testicles had been cut off.

Sada was a waitress at Ishida's restaurant; and the police soon put out a warrant for her and circulated her photograph to the press, which ran the details of the crime as front-page news. When she was finally arrested – having written two letters of farewell, as well as a long emotional message to her dead lover, as it turned out – the newspapers printed special editions. Sada was suddenly the hottest story in the entire country.

Sada Abe was the last child of a prosperous mat-maker in Kanda. But she was an incorrigible and promiscuous teenager, and at 18 her father sold her to a brothel in Yokohama as a geisha. She worked in the sex business, one way and another, through her twenties; and ended up in Tokyo as the kept woman of a rich middle-aged man. It was then – perhaps out of boredom, perhaps out of a need to earn extra cash – that she took a job as a waitress in Ishida's restaurant.

Ishida was married, with children, but he was also an inveterate womanizer; and it wasn't long before the two of them were secretly meeting for increasingly frenzied sex-sessions anywhere they could. Sada was insatiable – doctors later suggested she must have had a medical condition – but in Ishida she'd met her match. They began to push at the boundaries, obsessively searching out new ways to pleasure each other. She would throttle him with a sash cord to just this side of insensibility, so that a new flow of blood would travel to his penis, ballooning it and producing in both of them staggering, heartstopping orgasms. Finally, they went too far.

It's possible that a sedative Sada had bought for Ishida – who'd been complaining of insomnia – had weakened his resistance. But Sada, in interviews with the police, claimed that she'd meant to kill him. She said:

'I loved him so much, I wanted him all to myself... I knew that if I killed him no other woman could ever touch him again, so I killed him.'

About the cutting off of his genitals, she added:

'[They] belonged to someone I loved. Everything of Ishida's had become mine.'

Sada – who by then had spawned a new Japanese word, Sada-ism – was sentenced to six years imprisonment, but was released under an amnesty in 1941. She moved away from Tokyo under an assumed name, and got married. Then, in 1947, she was rediscovered by a journalist, and the whole story was retold in garish detail in a best-seller, *The Sex Confessions of Sada*. In a subsequent magazine interview with a well-known author, Sada said that she had only ever loved one man, Kichizo Ishida. The author later described what she'd done as:

'total love... for her to cut off his member as a keepsake was the ultimate feminine act.'

The last time Ishida's genitals were seen was at a post-war department-store exhibition sponsored by – among others – theDepartment of Health and Welfare. Since then a full-scale biography of Sada has appeared, as well as several films about her and Ishida's liaison: among them the erotic masterpiece of Nagisa Ōshima, *In the Realm of the Senses*.

IDI AMIN

WHEN MILTON OBOTE in 1962 became the first prime minister of newly-independent Uganda, he had to forge his country's forty independent tribes into a new national unity. This required finesse, but also, on occasion, brutality; and for brutality he increasingly relied on the deputy-commander of his army, a semi-literate ex-heavyweight champion and sergeant in the King's African Rifles: Idi Amin.

Amin was a Muslim from a minority tribe, an outsider with no loyalties to any particular power bloc – nor, indeed, to Obote. For in 1971, he took power himself in an army-led coup; and almost immediately started killing the officers who had helped him. Gathered together in groups under various pretexts, they were variously bayonetted to death, crushed by tanks or blown up by grenades thrown into rooms locked from the outside. The severed head of the murdered chief-of-staff found a home in Amin's freezer. When two Americans, one a journalist, got wind of this wholesale slaughter, they were simply disposed of.

Amin was soon demanding massive injections of cash from Britain and Israel. He got none; and within a year, with all its stocks of dollars and pounds reserved for Amin's own use, Uganda was bankrupt. Only money from Colonel Gadaffi in Libya kept it afloat – and this meant having to toe Libya's political line. Amin, then, began a prolonged tirade against the state of Israel. Israeli engineers working on construction projects were thrown out of the country; and an office of the Palestine Liberation Organization was opened in Kampala instead. Amin, warming to his task, started to express his profound admiration for Adolf Hitler; and even set up a domestic version of Hitler's Gestapo, the State Research Bureau, filled with hundreds of highly-paid killers.

Gadaffi's money, though, was not enough to guarantee the loyalty of all those Amin had to buy. So in August 1972, he announced that he'd had a visit from God; and God had told him that Uganda's Asian population, most of them professionals, merchants and shopkeepers, were at the root of the country's economic troubles. He gave them ninety days to leave the country; and when they fled, he handed over their businesses and shops to his cronies – who inevitably ran them into the ground. Once more they had to be paid; and the only commodity Amin had left to deal in was the lives of his fellow Ugandans.

Ugandans have a profound respect for the bodies of their dead – and this is what Amin began to trade on. His State Research Bureau were licensed to kill anyone they chose, and then to offer their services to their victims' families as body-finders for as large a fee as they could charge. The families were told that their sons or husbands had been arrested and were feared dead. They were then led, sometimes hundreds of them at night, to the dumping-grounds, in a forest outside Kampala. (Unclaimed – and therefore profitless – bodies were simply dumped into Lake Victoria.)

When the French Embassy complained about the constant gunfire coming from the Research Bureau's headquarters, Amin and his Bureau chief invented a new variation of the production line: one kidnapped prisoner was offered his life in return for bludgeoning another to death with a sledgehammer. Then he took the second prisoner's place...

It was only with the famous raid at Entebbe airport – when Israeli commandos rescued the passengers of an El Al aircraft hijacked by Palestinian gunmen – that Amin was finally exposed as an international pariah, and his reign of terror came to an end. Even then, though, he had one more trick up his sleeve. In a last attempt to get the support of his countrymen, he announced that Tanzania was getting ready to invade, an invasion that he did his best to provoke by sending raiders across the border into Tanzanian territory. When the Tanzanians did finally respond by sending their army into Uganda, it was welcomed with open arms. Amin fled to Libya, and then subsequently to a private hotel suite in Riyadh in Saudi Arabia, courtesy of the Saudi royal family. He died, still in exile, in 2003.

COUNTESS ELIZABETH BATHORY

WHEN COUNTESS ELIZABETH Bathory, aged 15, married Count Nadasdy in around 1576, it was an alliance between two of the greatest dynasties in Hungary. For Nadasdy, the master of Castle Csejthe in the Carpathians, came from a line of warriors, and Elizabeth's family was even more distinguished: It had produced generals and governors, high princes and cardinals – her cousin was the country's prime minister. Long after they've been forgotten, though, she will be remembered. For she was an alchemist, a bather in blood – and one of the models for Bram Stoker's Dracula.

She was beautiful, voluptuous, savage – a fine match for her 21-year-old husband, the so-called 'Black Warrior'. But he was forever off campaigning, and she remained childless. More and more, then, she gave in to the constant cajolings of her old nurse, Ilona Joo, who was a black witch, a satanist. She began to surround herself with alchemists and sorcerers; and when she conceived – she eventually had four children – she may have been finally convinced of their efficacy. For when her husband died, when she was about 41, she surrendered to the black arts completely.

There had long been rumours around the castle of lesbian orgies, of the kidnappings of young peasant women, of flagellation, of torture. But one day after her husband's death, Elizabeth Bathory slapped the face of a servant girl and drew blood; and she noticed that, where it had fallen on her hand, the skin seemed to grow smoother and more supple. She was soon convinced that bathing in and drinking the blood of young virgins would keep her young forever. Her entourage of witches and magicians – who were now calling for human sacrifice to make their magic work – agreed enthusiastically.

Elizabeth and her cronies, then, began scouring the countryside for children and young girls, who were either lured to the castle or kidnapped. They were then hung in chains in the dungeons, fattened and milked for their blood before being tortured to death and their bones used in alchemical experiments. The countess, it was said later, kept some of them alive to lick the blood from her body when she emerged from her baths, but had them, in turn, brutally killed if they either failed to arouse her or showed the slightest signs of displeasure.

Peasant girls, however, failed to stay the signs of ageing, and after five years Elizabeth decided to set up an academy for young noblewomen. Now she bathed in blue blood, the blood of her own class. But this time, inevitably, news of her depravities reached the royal court; and her cousin, the prime minister, was forced to investigate. A surprise raid on the castle found the Countess in mid-orgy; bodies lying strewn, drained of blood; and dozens of girls – some flayed and vein-milked, some fattened like Strasbourg geese awaiting their turn – in the dungeons.

Elizabeth's grisly entourage was taken into custody and then tortured to obtain confessions. At the subsequent trial for the murder of the 80 victims who were actually found dead at the castle, her old nurse, Ilona Joo, and one of the Countess's procurers of young girls, were sentenced to be burned at the stake after having their fingers torn out; many of the rest were beheaded. The Countess, who as an aristocrat could not be arrested or executed, was given a separate hearing in her absence at which she was accused of murdering more than 600 women and children. She was then bricked up in a tiny room in her castle, with holes left only for ventilation and the passing of food. Still relatively young and curiously youthful, she was never seen alive again. She is presumed to have died – since the food was from then on left uneaten – four years later, on 21 August 1614.

JEAN BEDEL BOKASSA

TO THE FRENCH who'd once ruled the Central African Republic, Colonel Jean Bedel Bokassa must at first have seemed a good bet. For it was soon clear, after he seized power in 1966, that he longed to be more French than they. He worshipped De Gaulle and Napoleon and tried to set up in his capital of Bangui the sort of art, ballet and opera societies characteristic of a French provincial town. He made concessions to French companies; allowed the French army a base; and entertained French president Giscard d'Estaing several times on his own private game reserve, which occupied most of the eastern half of the country. He was also extremely generous with gifts – particularly of diamonds, one of the few commodities his dirt-poor country produced.

By 1977, though, even the French must have begun to suspect that this ugly, violent little man was beginning to lose touch with reality. For, spurred on by constant viewings of a film of the coronation of Britain's Queen Elizabeth II, he'd decided to emulate his hero Napoleon and have himself crowned emperor. He'd even ordered a dozen prisoners held in Bangui Jail to be released from the general prison population and given exercise and proper rations in the run-up to the $20 million show.

French diplomats and businessmen, for all this, were among those who gratefully accepted invitations, and they were welcomed by brand-new Mercedes limousines paid for via a French government credit. They attended the comic-opera coronation and after the ceremonial parade – in which Bokassa rode in a gold carriage drawn by eight white horses over the only two miles of paved road in his capital – they assembled at his palace for a banquet, little knowing that among the delicacies served up to them on specially-ordered Limoges porcelain were what remained of the Bangui Jail prisoners...

It still took the French two years to move against Bokassa, who by that time had run mad. He'd become obsessed, for example, by the fact that the barefoot children of Bangui's only high school had no 'civilized' French-style uniforms. So he jailed them and then had them one by one

Bokassa allegedly fed his enemies to his pet crocodiles.

beaten to death when they failed to show up at 'uniform inspections' properly dressed. When news of this reached the French Embassy, they were finally forced to act. As Bokassa was leaving his 'Empire' for a state visit to Libya, an opposition politician was shaken awake in Paris and bundled on a plane to Bangui, where he called upon the French Foreign Legion troops who were hard upon his heels to 'aid the people' in Bokassa's overthrow.

The legionnaires soon uncovered the mass grave where the schoolchildren had been buried in the grounds of Bangui Jail. The bones of another 37 were found at the bottom of the swimming pool in Bokassa's palace – they'd been fed to his four pet crocodiles. In the palace kitchen were the half-eaten remains of another dozen victims who'd been on the emperor's menu in the days before his departure.

Bokassa first took refuge in the Ivory Coast in West Africa. But he soon showed up in a chateau in a Parisian suburb, where he entered a new career as a supplier of safari suits to African boutiques. President Giscard d'Estaing, meanwhile, made a personal donation to a Bangui charity school of $20,000 – which he said was the value of the diamonds Bokassa had given him.

CESARE BORGIA

OF THE BORGIAS, it is Lucrezia, perhaps, who has the worst reputation. But all she was was weak. It was her brother, the tyrant and murderer Cesare Borgia who seduced and tormented her, and then – mad with jealousy – scared off her first husband and murdered her second. After Cesare was wounded in battle and left to die, she lived a blameless life for another eleven years.

Cesare Borgia, like sister Lucrezia, was the bastard child of a courtesan and a cardinal who later, in 1492, became pope. He was immediately, aged 16, appointed Archbishop of Valencia; by 17, he was a cardinal. But it wasn't enough for the unscrupulous spoiled brat. For what he wanted was power: power over people, power over the affairs of state. Not for nothing was he the model of Niccolò Machiavelli's *The Prince*.

Power over people he satisfied sexually. He slept with every woman who attracted him, among them his sister and his brother's intended wife, and regularly had his homosexual partners either poisoned or assassinated. The Venetian ambassador later wrote:

> 'Every night four or five murdered men are discovered – bishops, prelates and others – so that all Rome is trembling for fear of being destroyed by the Duke Cesare.'

Power over the affairs of state, though, took more time. For elder brother Giovanni had been made head of the papal army and at the beginning of his reign the pope made a mistake: when the king of Naples died, he immediately recognized the king's son as his successor. Charles VIII of France, believing he himself had a better claim, promptly invaded; and the Borgias were forced into a humiliating retreat. Cesare was taken as a hostage, and though he subsequently escaped, he wanted personal revenge for the humiliations he'd suffered at the hands of the French court. He murdered all those he could find who had witnessed them; and then had a group of Swiss mercenaries who'd broken into his mother's house during the Frenchmen's stay in Rome tortured to death.

As far as the politics of state were concerned, however, fate soon played into his hands. For brother Giovanni disgraced himself in a campaign against the Orsini family, who'd collaborated with the French. So Cesare had him assassinated and – abandoning his church titles – took over Giovanni's role as his father's military and political right-hand man. Allied to the French again by now, and married to the king of Navarre's 16-year-old sister, he set about the business of bringing rebellious nobles into line and carving out a kingdom for himself in the area south of Venice.

As a commander, he was every bit as devious and ruthless as he had been as a cardinal. In one captured town he ordered 40 of the prettiest virgins to be brought to him for deflowering. In another, he demanded that its female ruler be brought to his bed – and wrote gloatingly to his father about what transpired. In yet another he promised to give safe passage to its young master in return for his surrender, only to have him sent to Rome and tortured to death. His friends and allies also suffered. He double-crossed the Duke of Urbino; had his own deputy hacked in two and displayed on a public square; and when he suspected disloyalty among those around him, invited them to a banquet and had them strangled.

Every time Cesare returned to Rome, the body count went up there. In 1500 he had sister Lucrezia's Neapolitan husband waylaid, and when he refused to die of his wounds, strangled him personally. He was also an adept poisoner – and it was poison, in the end, that brought him down. For in 1503 he and his father were invited by a cardinal to a banquet at a vineyard outside Rome. Both later became ill; his father died; and Cesare's life began to unravel. He was arrested and forced to give up his new kingdom. He fled to Naples, where he was again arrested, this time for disturbing the peace of Italy, and was sent to jail in Spain. He escaped once more to join the army of his brother-in-law, but after being wounded at a siege, he was recognized, stripped entirely naked and left to die of thirst.

ANDREI CHIKATILO

BETWEEN 1978 AND 1990, a serial sex murderer who became known as 'the Forest Strip Killer' terrorized the region around Rostov in southern Russia. When he was finally caught, he turned out to be a mild-mannered schoolteacher and Communist Party member called Andrei Chikatilo, who'd committed at least 53 murders – of women, children and drifters – over a period of 12 years. Chikatilo, though – who'd confessed to them all – was found guilty of only 52 of them. For another man had been executed for the first of his murders, that of a nine-year-old he'd lured into a rented shack at the age of 42.

That first killing of Chikatilo's, however, set the pattern for all the rest. For Chikatilo was impotent; and after choking the nine-year-old and attempting unsuccessfully to rape her, he ended up violating her with his fingers. It was the sight of the blood from her ruptured hymen that seems to have set him off. For he stabbed her repeatedly in what became a frenzy of sexual excitement; from then on power, blood, sex, torture and death became inseparably interlinked in his mind.

It was two years before he struck again – his victim this time a 17-year-old girl playing hookey from school who was willing to have sex for the price of a meal. He took her into the woods and beat her to death. Then he bit off one of her nipples and masturbated over her corpse.

From then on, the number of tortured and mutilated bodies began to pile up: older women, children and teenagers of both sexes. In 1984, Chikatilo was actually arrested by an investigating detective who noticed him behaving strangely on a bus. But though a rope, a long coil of wire and a knife were found in his briefcase, he was eventually released because his blood type didn't match that of the killer's. As it turned out, the bespectacled Chikatilo, fortunately for him, was a medical anomaly for his semen and blood type were different, AB and A. He was struck off the list of suspects.

He was finally caught, many brutal murders later, only in October 1990, when the last of his victims was found in woods near a remote country station. A policeman remembered asking a man he'd seen emerging nearby, dressed in a grey suit and with cuts to his finger and ear, for his identity. It was Chikatilo. He was first put under surveillance, and then pulled in. After several days' grilling, he confessed.

Put on trial in April 1992, he had no excuses – though he did mention that he'd seen his elder brother eaten by his neighbours in the Ukraine during the famine of the 1930s. He said:

'When I used my knife, it brought psychological relief. I know I have to be destroyed. I understand. I was a mistake of nature.'

He was executed, by a single gunshot behind the right ear, on Valentine's Day in 1994.

Chikatilo always professed his guilt once he was captured.

JOSEF FRITZL

JOSEF FRITZL WAS a strict father – a product, he would claim, of the Nazi-controlled Third Reich in which he grew up – but a good one, or so it seemed. An electrical engineer, he lived with his wife Rosemarie in their normal, provincial townhouse in the small Austrian town of Amstetten, where they brought up their seven children. But behind closed doors, he was a manipulative sociopath, driven to exert his power over others, patriarchal or otherwise, at any cost. In fact, he had already served a prison sentence, back in 1967, for raping a woman at knifepoint – a conviction which, conveniently for him, had been wiped from his record 15 years later in accordance with Austrian law. It was this mixture of outward respectability, fierce domination and legal loopholes that allowed the so-called 'Monster of Amstetten' to continue his reign of terror for nearly a quarter of a century. It was a horror story that was to ignite an international media furore and send shockwaves through local and national communities alike.

Elisabeth Fritzl was only 11 years old when her father's sexual abuse began. As she entered her teens, she began to rebel, staying out till the small hours and drinking and smoking in bars. She was stubborn and strong-willed to boot – which Fritzl didn't like one bit. He would later explain:

> 'That is why I had to do something; I had to create a place where I could keep Elisabeth, by force if necessary, away from the outside world.'

By the time she was 18, and no more disposed towards obedience, Fritzl had done just that. In fact, his meticulous planning of the kidnap and incarceration of his daughter had begun years in advance: he had built a secret basement and converted it into a prison cell up to three years earlier. Kitted out with just a washbasin, toilet, bed, hot plate and refrigerator, the dank, windowless dungeon was no luxury apartment. Fritzl had had the useful foresight to soundproof the 35 m^2 (377 sq feet) area and install huge, electronically-locking doors weighing up to 500 kg (1,110 lb), which he hid behind shelves in his basement workshop. A total of eight doors needed to be unlocked to reach the innermost cells. Clearly, Fritzl's plans were well-laid to the last detail.

On 29 August 1984, Fritzl lured Elisabeth into the basement, drugged her with ether, and locked her in the tiny concealed cellar. It would mark the last time in 24 years Elisabeth would see daylight. Upstairs, Fritzl told his wife Rosemarie that their daughter had run away to join a religious sect. It was not entirely beyond belief: Elisabeth had already run away from her unhappy, abusive home twice before. Submissive Rosemarie accepted her husband's explanation without question.

Elisabeth's father would visit the cellar regularly – once every three days or so – to bring food and supplies, and, before long, to have sex with his captive daughter, sometimes using chains to prevent her struggling. Over the course of her imprisonment Elisabeth was raped an estimated 3,000 times. Unsurprisingly, it was not long before she was impregnated. The first pregnancy miscarried; the second resulted in the birth of Kerstin in 1989. Between 1989 and 2002, Fritzl fathered seven of his daughter's children. One child, Michael, died three days after birth: when Fritzl saw the baby struggling to breathe, he told his anguished daughter, 'What will be, will be', and went upstairs to eat his dinner. After the baby's death, he incinerated the body in a stove in his cellar.

Of the six surviving children, three remained with Elisabeth in the basement. The other three, seemingly picked at random, Fritzl took upstairs one by one at birth and left them on the doorstep of his own house, each time with a note 'from Elisabeth' to express her wish for Rosemarie to bring them up. Once again, no questions were asked by family, friends or, indeed, the state. The 'upstairs children', fostered and later adopted by Josef and Rosemarie, were intelligent and well adjusted, oblivious to their mother and siblings living beneath them in tiny, dark quarters, threatened with gassing and electrocution if they tried to escape and ruled by fear of, and dependence on, their despotic father.

And so might Fritzl's terrifying domination have continued, but for Kerstin's sudden illness in April 2008. A desperate Elisabeth begged her father to allow the critically ill and unconscious 19-year-old to be removed from the cellar and taken to hospital for treatment. Fritzl agreed, explaining on arrival to sympathetic doctors that Kerstin had been left on his doorstep in this condition by his errant, absentee daughter. A week later, he even allowed Elisabeth a hospital visit to Kerstin, who had been diagnosed with kidney failure. Local police, acting on a tip-off, brought Elisabeth in for questioning. It was only after assurances she would never have to lay eyes on her father again that she began to reveal the horrific details of her captivity.

The ordeal was at last over, but the aftermath continues. The three 'downstairs children' suffered vitamin D deficiency, anaemia, illiteracy, agoraphobia and countless other issues linked to their incarceration; the three 'upstairs children' must come to terms with the breakdown of their adoptive family, their new relationship with their mother and the guilt that they did not suffer the traumas of those underground. All six are at high risk of genetic disease generated by the incest from which they were born. All have been given new identities. Life for the Fritzls will never again be normal.

It took a jury just three and a half days to find Josef Fritzl guilty of murder, rape, enslavement and incest. During the trial, the court heard that he knew he was 'born to rape' and chose Elisabeth, of his seven children, as his victim because:

'She was most like me. She was as stubborn as me, as strong as me. The stronger your opponent, the bigger the victory.'

When the 73-year-old was handed his life sentence, it seemed he had accepted that the remainder of his life would be spent firmly under lock and key. It is perhaps a fitting end for the tyrant who subjected his family to the same fate for so many years. His cell, though, has the luxury of a window.

FRITZ HAARMANN

EVERYONE SEEMED TO agree that Fritz Haarmann, though a bit simple-minded, was a genial sort: quick to offer advice or a loan to fellow-criminals and politeness itself to the police. He always came quietly when arrested; he was a model prisoner; and even when he became a police spy – playing both ends against the middle – he was so much part of the Hanover milieu by that time that no one seemed to notice or much mind. The social workers, trying to deal with all the homeless kids pouring into the city in the aftermath of the First World War, knew him and liked him: they thought of him as an ally. So did the porters at the railroad station, the market traders who bought second-hand clothing from him, and the housewives who oohed-and-aahed over the cheapness of his meat. No one at all had a bad word to say about Fritzi – until, that is, he was arrested in 1924 as one of the most horrific mass-murderers in European history. And even then the judges allowed him to interrupt witnesses and smoke a cigar in court.

Haarmann was born in 1879 in Hanover, and grew up a wanderer, a scrounger and petty thief – always in trouble with the law for pickpocketing and fraud and, on at least one occasion, sex offences with children. In 1913, the cops threw the book at him: he was sent to prison for five years; and by the time he emerged, the First World War had come and gone and Germany had plunged into chaos. Whole populations were on the move; the countryside and towns were full of homeless, rootless people, many of them teenage runaways desperate for a place to stay and work. Crime was universal; the black markets were thriving; people would buy and sell anything, without too many questions asked.

It was in this atmosphere that Haarmann, once out of prison, quietly set up a business as a meat-trader and dealer in second-hand clothes. Desperate for help against the rising tide of crime, the police soon recruited him as a spy – with the understanding that they wouldn't look too closely at whatever he was up to in return. So the universally popular Haarmann was free to go about his business – which involved hanging out with vagrant teenagers at the railroad station, taking them home for a meal or a bed and turning them into part of the food chain.

His relationship with the police was an effective cover: on one occasion, when forced to search his apartment, they gave it only a cursory look – and failed to notice the human head behind the oven. But so was his new profession as a butcher: the neighbours got used to the sounds of chopping, the bloodstained clothes and even a pail of blood carried down the stairs. Besides, Fritzi's meat was so good.

In September 1919 – with the butchery and the second-hand-clothes business both doing well – Haarmann acquired a partner: a cold, tyrannical 20-year-old called Hans Grans, who encouraged him to expand. The stream of boys and young men disappearing into the apartment they took together steadily grew – and so did the number of parents, arriving from other districts of Hanover or from outside the city, looking for their children – who were, of course, nowhere to be found. For their heads and bones had been tossed into the river Leine; and their meat had passed through the digestive systems of unsuspecting citizens.

From time to time through the early 1920s, someone would mention that Haarmann had been seen with one of the disappeared, or that Grans had been spotted wearing another's clothes. But by this time Haarmann had become indispensable to the police. He'd even set up a detective agency of his own with a high police official, and was recruiting for a secret organization which was plotting the violent removal of the French from the occupied Ruhr. Though ghastly rumours were by now beginning to sweep through Hanover, about werewolves, butchers and cannibals stalking through the night – and though Hanover was beginning to be seen in German newspapers as a monster, an eater of children – still nothing was done.

Then, though, in May 1924, two human skulls were found in the river Leine and the police chief was finally forced to deal, not only with public outrage, but also with the pile of circumstantial evidence that by now linked the police's favourite informer to the missing. He called in two detectives from Berlin and told them to follow Haarmann. They did, and promptly caught him attacking a teenager at the railroad station. He was arrested, and then his and Grans's apartment was searched. Faced with the evidence – of blood on the walls and second-hand clothes that could be linked to the disappeared – Haarmann confessed. More than a quarter of a tonne of bones and skulls was later retrieved from the river.

Haarmann had invariably butchered his prey, he said at his trial, by tearing their throats out with his teeth. He'd almost certainly had sex with and mutilated them further before finally carving them up. He said he couldn't remember how many victims there had been, perhaps 30, perhaps 40. But investigators believed that he killed 138 in the past 16 months alone. The total may have been as high as 600.

On 19 December 1924, he was found guilty of the murder of 27 boys between the ages of 12 and 18. He was beheaded the next day. Grans, who on occasion had urged him to kill simply because he fancied a particular victim's clothes, was sentenced to life imprisonment, later reduced to 12 years.

IVAN THE TERRIBLE

IVAN THE TERRIBLE was born under a bad star. When his father, the Grand Duke of Muscovy, divorced his first wife in 1525 to marry Ivan's mother, the patriarch of Jerusalem is said to have said:

'If you do this evil thing, you shall have an evil son. Your nation shall
become prey to terror and tears.'

Terror and tears it duly got. For even in his lifetime Ivan became known as,
not 'the Terrible' – a poor translation – but 'the Dread.'

By the time he was eight years old, Ivan was an orphan – his father dead
of an ulcer, his mother poisoned; and from then on, he later claimed, he
had 'no human care from any quarter.'

He grew up into a violent teenager – his first political act was to have
one of the leaders of the warring factions beneath him assassinated and
thrown to the dogs. Thirty of his followers were then hanged. One account
says that Ivan liked to throw animals down from the Kremlin walls just to
see them die; and that in the evenings – though full of daytime piety – he
rampaged through the streets of Moscow with a gang of friends, beating
up anyone who got in his way.

In 1547, Ivan had himself crowned as Tsar – Caesar – of all Russia,
and shortly afterwards married Anastasia, the 15-year-old daughter of an
influential member of his nobles' council.

She seems to have had a restraining influence on him; until she died
13 years later, he was a benevolent, if tough, ruler. He instituted reforms,
attacked corruption, gave his people wider representation and access to the
courts and reined in the powers of provincial governors. He also, by taking
back territory from the Tatars, the descendants of the Mongol Khans,
turned Russia into an imperial power.

In 1560, though, Anastasia died. Ivan soon imprisoned or exiled his
closest advisers and became increasingly violent and irrational. In 1564,
he withdrew from the capital completely and announced that he had laid
down the office of Tsar. A deputation of churchmen and nobles rode out
to see him and begged him to change his mind. He agreed, but only on
condition that from now on he be allowed to govern without interference,
and would have a free hand in dealing with traitors.

At this point he began a bizarre social experiment. He divided the
country into two halves, one of which was to be governed traditionally,
and the other of which was from now on to be his personal domain. In
his own half he soon unleashed the dark riders of a secret-service and
assassination squad, the *oprichniki*, who instituted a reign of terror, wiping

out all opposition to Ivan, killing more or less at will. Whole families were extirpated. Even the head of the Orthodox Church in Moscow was brutally murdered, while Ivan spent his time outside the capital, living a lifestyle, in the words of one historian,

'blended of monastic piety, drunken debauchery and bizarre cruelty.'

The climax of the terror came in 1570, when the citizens of Novgorod were accused of being ready to hand their city over to the Poles. Ivan immediately rode northward, completely destroying the countryside in every direction. Then he built a wooden wall around the city, and for five weeks engaged in indiscriminate slaughter. Children were tortured in front of their parents – and vice versa. Women were impaled on stakes or roasted on spits; men were used in spear-hunts or fried alive in giant skillets. Tens of thousands were killed, and when Ivan was done, he rode back to Moscow for more execution-by-torture, this time of many of his advisers, in Red Square. So awesome did his reputation become that later when he invaded Livonia, one town garrison blew itself up rather than fall into his hands. He tortured to death all those who survived.

In 1572, Ivan abandoned the division of this kingdom to beat off a Tatar invasion that threatened Moscow. By now, in any case, all opposition to him had been emasculated. From now on, as in his youth, he see-sawed between monkish piety and unbridled carnality and rage. In 1581, after finding his son and heir Ivan's pregnant wife not properly dressed, he threw her to the ground and kicked her. Then he lashed out at Ivan and fractured his skull. Both died within a few days.

By the time of Ivan's own death, after seven marriages and innumerable mistresses, he was raddled with disease. As a British trader put it:

'The emperor began grievously to swell in his cods [genitals], with which he had most horribly offended above fifty years, boasting of a thousand virgins he had deflowered and thousands of children of his begetting destroyed.'

In March 1584, acting in character, he called together 60 astrologers and told them to predict the day of his death, adding that if they got it wrong, they'd be burned alive. They said 18 March – and luckily for them he died one day before, before they could be proved wrong.

BÉLA KISS

BÉLA KISS WAS 40 years old when he moved with his young bride Mária to the Hungarian village of Czinkota in 1913. A plumber by trade, but obviously well-to-do, he bought a large house with an adjoining workshop and settled down to a quiet life, growing roses and collecting stamps. From time to time he would drive into Budapest on business, but otherwise his was an uneventful life. No one in the village ever thought to tell him that whenever he was away his wife was often seen out with a young artist called Paul Bihari.

Nor did anybody particularly remark on the fact that when he returned from the big city he started bringing oil drums back with him. Everyone, after all, knew that war was coming, and that fuel was likely to be scarce. When Kiss's wife and the artist Bihari ended up disappearing from Czinkota, the villagers took it for granted that they'd eloped. Why, Kiss even had a letter from his wife that said as much.

Besides, poor man, he was clearly distraught at what had happened. He withdrew from village life – and it only became clear much later what the oil drums, which he continued from time to time quietly to bring back from Budapest, along with the occasional female overnight guest, were really for...

After war came in August 1914, the reclusive Kiss was conscripted. While he served in the army, his house remained empty, its taxes unpaid; and then, in May 1916, news arrived that he'd been killed in action. His house was sold at auction for the unpaid taxes, and bought by a local blacksmith, who found seven oil-drums behind sheets of corrugated iron in the workshop. One day he opened one of them. It was full of alcohol – as were the rest of the drums. But in each one floated the body of a naked woman. When police subsequently searched the garden, they found the pickled bodies of another 15 women, aged between 25 and 50, and that of a single young man. All of them had been garrotted.

It wasn't long before police in Budapest picked up Kiss's trail. He'd been placing advertisements in a newspaper, giving a post-office box number and claiming to be a widower anxious to meet a mature spinster or widow, with marriage in mind. Both the name and the address he'd given the newspaper proved false. But one of the payments he'd made to it had been by postal order, and when the signature on it was published in the press, a woman came forward and said it was that of her lover, Béla Kiss – and she produced a postcard sent from the front to prove it. When a photograph of Kiss was found and published in its turn, he was recognized as a frequent – and sexually voracious – visitor to Budapest's red-light district. He'd apparently been using the savings he'd persuaded his victims to withdraw – in advance of their marriage – to feed his constant need for sex.

Kiss was, of course, dead. So the case was closed. But then a friend of one of his victims swore she'd seen him one day in 1919 crossing Budapest's Margaret Bridge. Five years later a former French legionnaire told French police of a Hungarian fellow-soldier, with the same name as that used in Kiss's ads, who'd boasted of his skill at garrotting. In 1932, Kiss was again recognized, this time in Times Square in New York. Had he swapped his identity with a dead man at the front and got away with it?

ILSE KOCH

IN 1950, WHEN the 'Bitch of Buchenwald' Ilse Koch was finally tried for mass murder in a German court, she protested that she had no knowledge at all of what had gone on in the concentration camp outside Weimar. Despite the evidence of dozens of ex-inmates, she insisted:

'I was merely a housewife. I was busy raising my children. I never saw anything that was against humanity!'

As hundreds of people gathered outside the court shouted 'Kill her! Kill her!' she was sentenced to life imprisonment.

Ilse Koch was born in Dresden, and by the age of 17 she was a voluptuous blue-eyed blonde: the very model of Aryan womanhood – and every potential storm-trooper's wet dream. Enrolling in the Nazi Youth Party, she went to work in a bookshop that sold party literature and under-the-counter pornography and she was soon having a string of affairs with SS men. Then, though, she came to the attention of SS and Gestapo chief Heinrich Himmler, who selected her as the perfect mate for his then top aide, the brutish Karl Koch. Shortly after the wedding, when Koch was appointed commander of Buchenwald, she was installed in a villa near the camp, given two children, and then more or less forgotten by her husband, who was too busy staging multiple sex-orgies in Weimar to care.

Perhaps in revenge, Ilse began mounting orgies of her own, taking five or six of her husband's officers into her bed at a time. She was perverse, sexually insatiable – and it wasn't long after the beginning of the war that she started turning her attention to the mostly Jewish prisoners at the camp.

She first sunbathed nude outside the wire to tantalize them; then started greeting their trucks and transport trains semi-naked, fondling her breasts and shouting obscenties. If any of the incoming prisoners looked up at her, they were beaten senseless; on one occasion, about which she filled out a report, two were clubbed to death and one had his face ground into the earth until he suffocated. All were executed, she wrote blithely, for ogling her.

She encouraged the guards to use the prisoners for target practice – and often took part herself. She scouted out good-looking soldiers seconded to the camp and offered them mass-orgies with her. Then, finally – perhaps jaded with mere sex – she started to collect trophies...

One day, by chance, she saw two tattooed prisoners working without their shirts. She ordered them to be killed immediately and their skins prepared and brought to her. She soon became obsessed with the possibilities of human skin, particularly if tattooed. She had lampshades made from the skin of selected prisoners for her living room, even a pair of gloves. Not content with this, she also started to experiment with prisoners' severed heads, having them shrunk down by the dozen to grapefruit size to decorate her dining-room.

She was tried as a war criminal at Nuremberg after the war by an American military court, and sentenced to life in prison, but two years later she was released, on the grounds that a crime by one German against others could not properly be considered a war crime. By the time she appeared in a German court in Augsburg, she was a bloated, raddled figure who blamed everything on her husband – who had conveniently been executed by the Nazis for embezzlement years before. She staged an epileptic fit in court, and when she heard its final judgment in her prison cell, she merely laughed. She hanged herself in Aichach Prison in 1967.

JOACHIM KROLL

IT WASN'T UNTIL July 1959 that German police began to recognize the signature of the man they came to call 'the Ruhr Hunter', Joachim

Kroll. For it was only then that he began cutting strips of flesh from his victims' bodies to take them home and cook them – and sometimes he couldn't be bothered to do any butchery at all if they were old and tough. When he was finally caught in 1976, he confessed to a total of 14 murders over a 22-year period. But there could well have been many more. For Kroll, though entirely cooperative, was a simpleton with not much of a memory – and what little he had, had to be jogged. He did, though, finally exonerate two men who'd been arrested for his murders and then released for lack of evidence. Of these two, one had been divorced by his wife and had then committed suicide; the other had been ostracized by his neighbours for six long years.

He'd started, Kroll told police, in 1955 at the age of 22. Too self-conscious and nervous for a real relationship – and dissatisfied with the rubber dolls he mock-strangled and masturbated over at home – he'd beaten unconscious, then raped and killed a 19-year-old girl in a barn near the village of Walstedde. Four years later, in a different part of the Ruhr, he struck again in exactly the same way, after tracking the movements of another young girl for some days.

A month later, in July 1959, he added the special signature which the police came to recognize after they found the body of a 16-year-old with steaks cut from her thighs and buttocks. The signature appeared again on the bodies of two more young girls within six weeks of each other in 1962, and then on a four-year-old in 1966. Kroll went on to rape and kill at least four more women and girls in the next ten years, but it wasn't until 1976, when a four-year-old disappeared from a playground in Duisburg, that his trademark reappeared in particularly grisly fashion.

The young girl had been seen wandering away from the playground with a mild-looking man she called 'uncle'. The police quickly started making a door-to-door enquiry, and were told something odd by a tenant in a nearby apartment building. He said he'd just been told by the janitor, Joachim Kroll, not to use one of the building's lavatories because it was stopped up. 'What with?' he'd asked; and Kroll had answered, 'Guts...'

A plumber was called, and soon found that Kroll had been exactly right: the lavatory had indeed been blocked by the intestines and lungs of a small child. When the police searched Kroll's apartment, they found human flesh wrapped in bags in the freezer, and on the stove, among the carrots and potatoes of a stew, the child's hand.

Kroll was a model prisoner. He seemed to think he'd be able to go home after he'd had an operation of some kind. So he readily confessed to all the murders he could remember – and he also told the police about two occasions on which he might have been caught. As for the human flesh, he hadn't taken it, he said, for any particularly sinister reason. He just thought he'd save money on meat...

PETER KÜRTEN

PETER KÜRTEN, THE so-called 'Vampire of Düsseldorf', was an indiscriminate murderer: he attacked and killed everything – men, women, children, animals – that came his way. Yet he was described by a psychiatrist at his trial in 1930 – where, from behind the bars of a specially-built cage, he spelled out the details of his crimes in meticulous detail – as a clever, even rather a nice man.

That he should have been so is astonishing. For Kürten's father had been a drunken, pathological sadist, who was sent to prison for repeatedly raping his wife and 13-year-old daughter and he himself had committed his first murders – the drowning of two playmates – at the age of nine. At about the same time, he later said, he was inducted by the local dog-catcher into the delights of torturing animals – he sometimes decapitated swans to drink their blood.

By the age of 16, he was a petty young hoodlum and occasional arsonist living in a ménage-à-trois with a masochistic older woman and her teenage daughter. He was arrested and sent to prison twice – first for theft and fraud, and then for deserting from the army the day after he'd been called up. In between these two sentences, though, while making his living as a burglar in Cologne-Müllheim, he committed his first murder as an adult, when he came across a ten-year-old girl in a room over an inn, throttled her and cut her throat with a pocket-knife.

'I heard the blood spurt and drip beside the bed,'

– he said calmly at his trial 17 years later.

His second sentence, for desertion, kept Kürten out of circulation, perhaps luckily, for eight years; and in 1921, when he came out, he seemed on the face of it a changed man. He got married in Altenburg, took a job in a factory and became known in the community as a quiet, well-dressed and charming man, active in trade union politics. Then, though, in 1925, Kürten and his wife moved to Düsseldorf – and the opportunistic attacks on complete strangers began.

'The Vampire', as he soon became known, attacked people with either scissors or knives, in broad daylight, any time – as if inflamed by the idea and sight of blood. By 1929, he had struck 46 times and four of his victims had died; and now, far from stopping, he was beginning to step up the rate and violence of his attacks. On the evening of 23 August of that year, he strangled and cut the throats of two young sisters on their way back from a fair; 12 hours later, after offering to take a servant-girl to another fair, he attacked and stabbed her as they walked through woods nearby. For a while there was a lull, but then he attacked three people, a man and two women, within a single half-hour; later he bludgeoned a pair of serving women to death. Finally, on 27 November, he killed a five-year-old girl, slashing her body 36 times.

The city of Düsseldorf was by now in a state of panic. But again, for a while, nothing more was heard from 'The Vampire.' Then, on 14 May 1930, Maria Budlick, a young girl looking for work in the city, arrived from Cologne and was picked up at the station by a man who offered to show her the way to a women's hostel. When he tried to take her into a nearby park, though, she refused on the grounds that she didn't know who he was – he might even be 'The Vampire.'

While they were busy arguing, a second man stepped up and asked her whether she was all right.

This second man was charm itself, Maria later said, and, when the first man left, he offered her something to eat before taking her to the hostel.

She agreed, and after a glass of milk and a sandwich at his house, they duly took a tram to the edge of the city. Still believing she was on the way to the hostel, Maria began walking with him through the Grafenberg Woods. Then, suddenly, he said:

> 'Do you know where you are? You are alone with me in the middle of the woods. You can scream as much as you like and no one will hear you!'

He seized her by the throat and threw himself on her. She fought back; and then, quite unexpectedly, he let go of her, and asked her if she could remember where he lived. Maria, in fact, could remember, but she said no, she couldn't. Satisfied, the man then stood up and calmly showed her towards the woods' exit.

When the police found out about this incident – through a misaddressed letter Maria sent to a friend about it – they located her and asked her to take them to the house she'd visited. She did, and saw the man she'd met – Peter Kürten – going in. Kürten, having recognized her too, must have known immediately that his days of freedom were numbered. For he soon left, went to the restaurant where his wife worked and coolly confessed to her that he was 'The Vampire' – she could now claim the reward. A few days later, she went to the police and told them where he was.

The trial was a formality, consisting almost entirely of Kürten's detailed confessions to the nine murders and seven attempted murders he'd been charged with. Yes, he'd drunk blood. Yes, he was a sadist, an arsonist, a rapist, a vampire. He was sentenced to death nine times. On 1 July 1931, before his walk to the guillotine, he asked the prison psychiatrist whether he'd be able to hear, if only for a second, the gouting of his own blood as the blade cut through his neck. 'That,' he said, 'would be the greatest of all pleasures.'

HENRI LANDRU

HENRI LANDRU WAS a conman and a fraudster, specializing in lonely widows and spinsters; by 1914, when he was 45, he'd already been in prison four times for swindling and abuse of confidence. In 1914, though, he was in the dock again, and this time for something more serious: business fraud – for which he could expect four years in jail, followed by banishment to a faraway penal colony as a habitual criminal. So he went on the lam and changed his name, and seems to have made one more important decision: from now on, he'd kill his victims, rather than leave them alive to give evidence against him.

His first victim of this new resolution was a 39-year-old widow and her 18-year-old son. Calling himself Monsieur Diard, he moved them into a villa on the outskirts of Paris, where they both disappeared.

Another widow, this time Argentinian, soon followed them, bringing all her worldly possessions. She lasted five days.

By this time Landru had started placing lonely hearts advertisements in the newspapers of Paris, claiming to be a widower of 43, with 'a comfortable income,' 'moving in good society' and desirous 'to meet widow with a view to matrimony.' From this and six other ads which were to follow,

Henri Landru maintained his innocence right up until his execution.

he got almost 300 replies, which he recorded meticulously in a black notebook. One of them was his next prey: a 51-year-old ex-governess with a considerable legacy. When she disappeared, Landru, together with her legacy, moved to the Villa Ermitage near the village of Gambais – and this was to be the centre of his operations from then on.

The widows came – and went – over a period of almost three and a half years, leaving not even their identities behind them. But then the sisters of two of Landru's victims began making enquiries; and both separately wrote to the local mayor about the Villa Ermitage, where both sister-widows had gone to visit a man called, variously, 'Monsieur Dupont' and 'Monsieur Fremyet'. The mayor put the two of them together and a complaint was made to the police. Then, in April 1919, one of the sisters recognized 'Monsieur Fremyet' walking, with a young girl on his arm, in Paris's rue de Rivoli.

'Monsieur Fremyet' was arrested and the police found on him not only his black notebook, but also papers and identity cards belonging to some of the women on his list. In a stove at the Villa Ermitage, they later discovered fragments of human bone amongst the ashes – though they never managed to produce a corpse, however long and hard they dug.

Landru, once he'd been identified, said nothing, except to profess his innocence. His trial, though, when it came, was a sensation. For the police had put it about by then that he'd killed 300 women, perhaps more. He was tried for just ten of them, and for the murder of his first victim's son, and was found guilty – via circumstantial evidence, proven motive and the evidence provided by the Villa Ermitage stove – on all counts. On 30 November 1921, still maintaining his innocence, he walked to the guillotine with some hauteur, refusing the ministrations of a priest. But more than 40 years later, the daughter of Landru's lawyer found a confession he'd written and hidden on the back of a picture he'd drawn whilst awaiting his execution.

'LUCKY' LUCIANO

MORE PERHAPS THAN any other single man, 'Lucky' Luciano created the modern face of the Mafia: making vast profits from drugs, operating across borders, invisible; bolstered by international agreements and alliances and ruled by representative councils. An associate once said of him and his long-time friend Meyer Lansky:

> 'If they had been President and Vice-President of the United States, they would have run the place far better than the idiot politicians.'

Salvatore Lucania arrived in New York with his parents at the age of 10 – and was almost immediately in trouble, for theft and later drug-peddling. Then, in his early twenties, he met and became the mentor of a young Polish immigrant called Maier Suchowjansky, better known as Meyer Lansky. By that time, Luciano was a member of the gang run by Jacob 'Little Augie' Orgen, a union and organized-labour racketeer, and was making himself a reputation as a hit-man. Lansky was soon co-opted into the gang as a strategist during the early days of Prohibition, though he'd have nothing to do with the brothels Luciano ran on the side.

It wasn't long, however, before they outgrew Orgen's gang and looked for new opportunities, together with a friend of Luciano's called Vito Genovese. Prohibition made the three of them increasingly powerful. Luciano later claimed that he personally controlled every New York police precinct and had a bagman deliver $20,000 a month to Police Commissioner Grover A. Whelan. He also boasted about the company he moved in: the politicians and stars he met at parties and the gatherings at the Whitney estate. The politicians, even presidential candidates, courted him for campaign funding and help at election time. The beautiful people wooed him for World Series baseball tickets, girls, dope and drink.

There remained one major obstacle, though, to Luciano's assumption of absolute power. For the most important criminal power-brokers in New York, even during Prohibition, were two old-style Mafia bosses, Salvatore Maranzano and Giuseppe Masseria. Luciano favoured Masseria, but he soon changed his mind when Maranzano had him picked up, strung up by his thumbs and tortured. The final inducement to change allegiances was a slash across the face from a knife held by Maranzano which needed 55 stitches. The reward? The Number Two spot in the Maranzano outfit if Luciano first killed Masseria.

Masseria was gunned down in the middle of dinner in a Coney Island restaurant, after Luciano, his dining partner, had left for the bathroom; Maranzano proclaimed himself the *Capo di Tutti Capi* at a meeting of the New York Mafia families, which he proposed to bring together under one roof as La Cosa Nostra. Luciano and Lansky, though, had other ideas. And a few months later, four of their men, posing as internal-revenue investigators, arrived at Maranzano's Park Avenue headquarters, demanding to see both the boss and the books. Maranzano was stabbed and shot to death in his inner office.

In victory, Luciano took over Maranzano's idea. He established the New York Commission – sometimes known as the National Crime Syndicate – and its enforcement arm, Murder Incorporated. He became, in effect, the boss of bosses; and even though he was jailed in 1936 for 25 to 50 years, on vice charges, he continued to exercise power. For after the United States entered the war, the government needed help, first against sabotage in the Mafia-controlled New York docks, and then with the invasion of Sicily.

Luciano agreed, in return for early release after the war ended. Pro-Mussolini Italian spies and saboteurs were flushed out; German spies were quietly assassinated; and when the US Army landed in Sicily, special units carried, not only the Stars and Stripes, but a special flag carrying the letter 'L.' The Mafia eased their path through the island, making sure that its members took over the running of the towns and villages they passed through. By the time the US Army moved onto the mainland, it had taken over virtually all of Sicily.

It was, in a way, Luciano's greatest coup, and when released and deported to Italy in 1945 – after making a huge donation, it's said, to the Republican Party – he took full advantage. After a brief interlude in Cuba, he settled in Naples, and from there organized in Sicily the setting up of the same sort of ruling Mafia commission he'd established in the United States. He also moved the Sicilian families into drugs; and is said to have established the so-called French Connection, an alliance between Turkish growers, the Sicilian families, Corsican gangster-processors in Marseilles and US Mafia importers and distributors.

His life finally caught up with 'Lucky' Luciano when he died on 26 January 1962 in Naples Airport after drinking a cup of coffee. He may have had a heart attack; he may have been poisoned. But it seems typical of the man that he was due to meet an American film producer who wanted to make a film of his life – and that there were Interpol agents, by report, keeping watch.

'COUNT' VICTOR LUSTIG

'COUNT' VICTOR LUSTIG, born in 1890 into a respectable Czecho-slovakian family, was an inveterate Lothario with a passion for gambling. But he was also the most famous conman of the 20th century. For the 'Count' was the man who successfully sold the Eiffel Tower – and not once, but twice.

Whether Victor Lustig was actually his real name no one ever really knew. For in his wanderings across Europe in the first quarter of the 20th century, he seems to have had 22 different aliases and to have been arrested 45 times under one or other of them. It was as Victor Lustig, though, that he had his brilliant idea. One day in 1925, he read in a Paris newspaper that the Eiffel Tower was in desperate need of renovation, and that it might even have to be demolished. In short order, then, he got hold of some headed notepaper from the Ministry of Posts, which was responsible for the Tower's maintenance, and sent out letters to five rich financiers, inviting them to a private meeting with the 'deputy director-general' of the Ministry at the Hotel Crillon.

At the meeting in a hotel suite, the financiers were told that the business they were about to discuss was top secret, hence the need for a discreet meeting with loyal Frenchmen at a venue outside the Ministry. The decision, regrettably, had been taken, he said, to pull the Eiffel Tower down, since it was now impossibly expensive to maintain. It was to be sold off for the value of its 7,000 tons of metal, he said; and he asked the five if they'd care to submit bids for it.

All agreed, but Lustig was only really interested in one of the bidders, a nouveau-riche scrap-metal merchant called André Poisson. So when the bids were in, he rang Poisson to tell him that his had been successful. Now, if he'd care to bring a certified cheque to the Hotel Crillon, the business could be concluded.

Poisson dutifully came to the hotel; whatever suspicions he might have had were allayed when Lustig apologetically asked for a further amount of money, in cash, to help smooth the wheels. Poisson immediately agreed and happily handed over the cheque, worth millions of francs, in return for a bill of sale. When a French ministry official asked for a bribe, after all, that clearly meant he was the real thing.

Lustig and a confederate he'd employed immediately left town, and stayed away until they realized that they'd got away with it: Poisson had been too embarrassed to go to the police. So they returned again to Paris, repeated the process, and sold the Eiffel Tower to another scrap-merchant. Though this dealer did finally go to the police, by that time they were already far away.

Lustig's career as a con-man was not over now by any means, but he never reached such dizzy heights again. He worked the transatlantic liners; sold a 'banknote-duplicating' machine to multi-millionaire Herbert Loller; and even tried to involve Al Capone in a Wall-Street investment scam. Then, in the early thirties, he went into counterfeit money. In 1934, he was arrested for producing $100,000-worth a month and thrown into New York's Tombs Prison. He escaped and went to ground in Pittsburgh. But after some years of life as retiring Robert Miller, the police were tipped off and he was rearrested, on a charge of having distributed an awesome $134 million-worth of fake bills over his career. He was sentenced to 20 years, first in Alcatraz and then in Springfield Prison, Missouri, where he died in 1947.

CHIZUO MATSUMOTO
(AKA SHOKO ASAHARA)

IN THE 1980s, a partially blind Japanese masseur called Chizuo Matsumoto (aka Shoko Asahara) claimed to have travelled to the Himalayas and to have achieved nirvana there – he said he could now levitate and even walk through walls. A group of believers gathered around him into an organization called AUM Supreme Truth and in spring 1989 they applied to the Tokyo Municipal Government for registration as a religion.

The bureaucrats had their doubts. For Asahara, as he preferred to call himself, had a police record for fraud and assault; and there were already complaints that AUM was abducting children and brainwashing them against their parents. In August, though, they caved in after demonstrations by AUM members, giving it not only tax-exempt status, but also the right to own property and to remain free of state and any other interference.

Less than three months later, a young human rights lawyer who had been battling the cult on behalf of worried parents vanished into thin air, along with his wife and infant son. It later transpired that a television company had shown an interview with the lawyer to senior AUM members before its transmission, but it hadn't bothered to tell the lawyer this. Nor did it bother to tell the police either, after the lawyer's disappearance.

In the period between 1989 and 1995, AUM hit the news in a variety of ways, mostly as a public nuisance. But the locals who protested its setting up of yoga schools and retreats in remote rural areas didn't know the half of it. For during these years AUM – which attracted many middle-class professionals – began using them to stockpile the raw materials used in making nerve agents: sarin and its even more deadly cousin VX. Its members tried to produce conventional weapons, AK-47s, but they also travelled deep into research on botulism and a plasma-ray gun. When in 1993 neighbours complained of a foul smell coming from an AUM building in central Tokyo, the police took no action. But then they weren't to know that scientists there were doing their best to cultivate anthrax.

Then on the night of 27 June 1994, in the city of Matsumoto 150 miles west of Tokyo, a man called the police complaining of noxious fumes, and subsequently became so ill he had to be rushed to hospital. Two hundred others became ill and seven died. Twelve days later, this time in Kamikuishiki-mura, a rural village 300 miles north of Tokyo, the same symptoms – chest pains, nausea, eye problems – reappeared in dozens of victims. And though this time no one died, the two attacks had something sinister in common. For the Matsumoto deaths, it was discovered, had been caused by sarin, hitherto unknown in Japan; and the village casualties by a by-product created in its manufacture.

The villagers were convinced that the gas had come from an AUM building nearby and by the beginning of 1995, the newspapers – if not the police – had begun to put two and two together. One paper reported that traces of sarin had been found in soil samples near another AUM retreat; another explained the attack on Matsumoto, for three judges who were to rule on a lawsuit brought against AUM lived in a building there next to a company dormitory where most of the casualties had occurred.

Still the police took no action. Nor did they move when in February a notary, a well-known opponent of the sect, was abducted in broad daylight in Tokyo by a van that could be traced to AUM. In early March, passengers on a Yokohama commuter train were rushed to hospital complaining of eye irritation and vomiting; and ten days later the method in which they'd probably been attacked was found. Three attaché cases – containing a liquid, a vent, a battery and small motorized fans – were discovered dumped at a Tokyo station.

Perhaps forewarned of a coming police raid, AUM took pre-emptive action. At the height of the morning rush hour on 25 March, cult members released sarin on three subway lines that converged near National Police headquarters. Twelve died and over 5,000 were injured. There was panic all over Japan. But, though the police did raid some AUM facilities the following day, they still failed to find Asahara and his inner circle. The price they paid was high. For on 30 March a National Police superintendent was shot outside his apartment by an attacker who got away on a bicycle. A parcel bomb was sent to the governor of Tokyo; cyanide bombs were found and defused in the subway system; and when a senior AUM figure was finally arrested, he was promptly assassinated, like Lee Harvey Oswald.

Through all this, Asahara and a number of his ministers were in almost daily touch with selected press. In fact he wasn't arrested, hiding out in a steel-lined room at AUM's compound at Kamikuishiki-mura, until almost two months after the Tokyo attack. And it was only very slowly, even then, that his motives and the extent of his crimes were unravelled.

The ex-masseur had started AUM Supreme Truth, it seems, for the money he could make and he early recruited members from another sect who knew the religion business. But then he'd become infected by his own propaganda and when sect members ran in national elections in 1990 – and lost in a big way – he decided to bring down the government in preparation for a final Armageddon that would take place in 1997. Everything he undertook from then on was bent to this single purpose. In an atmosphere of obsessive secrecy, he organized bizarre initiation rituals and assassinated or abducted anyone who stood in his way. He demanded that members give up their worldly goods to him and had them killed if they refused. He operated prostitution clubs, made deals with drug syndicates, and instigated break-ins at government research laboratories. . .

The full extent of his crimes is still not yet known. For the trials and appeals of both Asahara and his high officers continues. Meanwhile, so does his cult – under a new name Aleph. It's still remarkably popular.

JACQUES MESRINE

PRESIDENT GISCARD D'ESTAING regarded the failure to catch Jacques Mesrine as a national disgrace. Much of the rest of the population were delighted. For they sneakingly saw Mesrine as a combination of d'Artagnan, Robin Hood and Errol Flynn: a glorious example of France's daring and ingenuity. True, he might have killed a few times – and that was regrettable. But his wit! His escapes! His nerve! Besides, he was the most famous criminal in the world – and he was French! When he finally died in a police ambush in Paris in 1979, the police may have hugged each other and danced in the street, but there was something in the heart of every true Frenchman that mourned.

Mesrine was born in Paris in 1937 – and from his earliest years he seems to have been in love with danger. As a schoolboy he was laid back, fond of argument and good with his fists; as a teenager, he hung out with other tearaways and played hookey to go joyriding. For a while he tried marriage, but he couldn't settle down, and when he was conscripted into the army he specifically asked to be sent to Algeria, where the French army was fighting a 'dirty war' against Muslim anti-colonialists.

He was demobbed with a Military Cross for bravery. But life as a civilian – after seeing action – seemed to bore him. He committed his first burglary, on the flat of a wealthy businessman, in 1959 – and it bore all the hallmarks of what was to come. When a drill snapped as he was boring his way into the safe, he simply left, broke into a hardware store for more and came back to finish the job. He escaped with millions of francs.

His reputation rapidly spread in the underworld – and among the police. In 1962 he was arrested on his way to a bank job and sentenced to three years in prison. Out a year later, he tried to go straight: he got married again and apprenticed himself to an architect. But after showing real aptitude, he was made redundant, and he went back to the high-wire daring and near escapes of crime. Within four years he was the most wanted thief in France; the police were infuriated by his audacious antics. So, after one last major job at a hotel in Switzerland, he took himself off with his latest girlfriend, Jeanne Schneider, to Canada.

They were soon employed, as chauffeur and housekeeper, by a Montreal millionaire. But after rows with other staff, they were sacked. So Mesrine and Jeanne simply kidnapped the millionaire and held him for $200,000

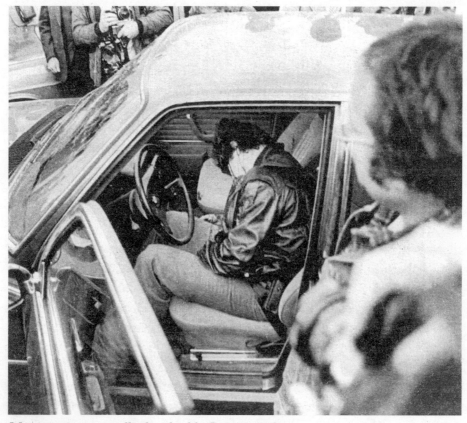

Mesrine was eventually shot dead by Parisian police.

ransom. Unfortunately they were caught and charged both with the kidnap and with the murder of a rich widow they'd befriended in the small town of Percé nearby.

From the beginning Mesrine was outraged: he insisted they'd had nothing to do with the widow's murder. (They were both eventually acquitted.) But he engineered his and Jeanne's escape from the Percé jail; and after they were caught again, and tried and sentenced for the kidnap, he organized another spectacular escape from the 'escape-proof' St. Vincent de Paul prison at Laval. (He later tried to go back to free the rest of the prisoners, but got into a gunfight with the police along the way.)

The escape made Mesrine a national celebrity in Canada, but his reputation darkened after he shot to death two forest rangers who'd recognized him. So finally, after some extraordinarily insouciant bank hold-ups – he robbed one bank twice because a cashier had scowled at him on the way out the first time – he decided to take the money, and a new mistress, to Venezuela.

In 1973, though, Mesrine was back in France and up to his old tricks. After a string of armed robberies, he was finally arrested. But he again escaped, this time from the Palais de Justice in Compiègne. By now, he was deep into his gentleman-thief, Robin-Hood role. When, during a bank robbery, a young woman cashier accidentally pushed the alarm button, he said,

'Don't worry, my dear. I like to work to music,'

and calmly went on gathering the money. On another occasion, when his father was in hospital, dying of cancer and closely watched, he simply dressed up as a doctor – with white coat and stethoscope – and went to visit him.

When he was finally arrested and then held in Santé Prison, he whiled away the time writing his autobiography. Then, when his case, after three and a half years, came to trial, he gave a demonstration in court that was to seal his reputation. After saying that it was easy enough to buy a key for any pair of handcuffs, he simply took out a key from a match-box hidden in the knot of his tie and opened his own handcuffs.

A year later, after being sentenced to 20 years, he escaped yet again, and continued his bizarre adventures. He walked into a Deauville police station, saying he was an inspector from the Gaming Squad, and asked to see the duty inspector. When told he was out, he took himself off and that night robbed a Deauville casino. He also invaded the house of a bank official who'd testified against him at his trial, and forced him to withdraw half a million francs from his own bank. He gave an interview to *Paris Match*, the first of several he gave to journalists; and he even then attempted to kidnap the judge who'd tried him. Though this went badly wrong, he escaped by telling the police whom he met on their way up the stairs: 'Quick, quick, Mesrine's up there.'

By the time he was finally caught up with, he was living with a girlfriend in a luxury apartment in Paris; and the police were in no mood to compromise. They staked out the apartment, and then when the couple came out and climbed into his BMW, they were soon hemmed in by two lorries. Unable to move, he was then shot – in effect, executed. The police thereupon kissed each other and danced in the street – and President Giscard d'Estaing was immediately informed of their triumph.

ROBERT PICKTON

ROBERT PICKTON LIVED on a pig farm, a muddy, run-down 17-acre parcel of land in Port Coquitlam that he and his siblings had inherited from their parents.

On the occasions that he left his home, Pickton could often be found 30 km (20 miles) away hunting down the drugged and desperate in Vancouver.

For runaways, the homeless and those who were simply down on their luck, British Columbia's biggest city holds an understandable allure. Nestled by the warm Pacific Ocean, it enjoys a much milder winter than any other major Canadian city. For the drug addict, there's a steady supply of illegal narcotics flowing through its port. For those who still dream of sudden fame, there is fantasy to be found in the city's film industry; 'Hollywood North' is just one of Vancouver's many nicknames.

This city, with the highest concentration of millionaires in North America, is also home to the poorest neighbourhood in the country. Haunted by glorious buildings, reminders of long-gone days as a premier shopping district, Vancouver's Downtown Eastside is now a blight on the landscape. The banks disappeared years ago, as did the well-stocked department

Pig farmer Robert Pickton.

stores. The few shops that aren't boarded up house lowly pawnbrokers. Outside their doors, and in the blocks that surround, prostitutes – some as young as 11 years old – ply their trade.

But Pickton did not prey on children. It's thought that his first victim was a 23-year-old woman named Rebecca Guno, who was last seen on 22 June 1983. She was reported missing three days later – a very short time period compared to the many that followed. The next victim, Sheryl Rail, was not reported missing for three full years.

The lives of Guno and Rail were just two of the six Pickton is known to have taken in his first decade of killing. With as much as 28 months separating one murder from the next, the pig farmer had no clear pattern. These early erratic and seemingly spontaneous killings enabled Pickton to pass under the radar. It wasn't until the closing years of the millennium that speculation began to surface that a serial killer just might be at work on the seedier streets of Vancouver. By then Pickton had picked up the pace; it's believed that he killed nine women in the latter half of 1997 alone.

The next year, the Vancouver Police Department began reviewing cases of missing women stretching back nearly three decades.

By this time, talk of a serial killer was a subject of conversation in even the most genteel parts of the city, and still the authorities dismissed speculation out of hand.

When one of their own, Inspector Kim Rossmo, raised the issue, he was quickly shot down. 'We're in no way saying there is a serial murderer out there,' said fellow inspector Gary Greer. 'We're in no way saying that all these people missing are dead. We're not saying any of that.'

The police posited that the missing women had simply moved on. After all, prostitutes were known to abruptly change locations and even names. Calgary, 970 km (600 miles) to the east and flush with oil money, was often singled out as a likely destination.

Years later, veteran journalist Stevie Cameron would add this observation: 'There were never any bodies. Police don't like to investigate any case where there isn't a body.'

Even as the authorities dismissed the notion of a serial killer, Pickton continued his bloody work. Among those he butchered was Marcella Creison. Released from prison on 27 December 1998, she never showed at a belated Christmas dinner prepared by her mother and boyfriend. Sadly, 14 days passed before her disappearence was reported.

The waters were muddied by the fact that some of the women who had been reported missing were actually found alive. Patricia Gay Perkins, who had disappeared leaving a one-year-old son behind, contacted Vancouver Police after reading her name on a list of the missing. One woman was found living in Toronto, while another was discovered to have died of a heroin overdose. However, the list of missing women continued to grow, even as other cases were solved.

Accepting, for a moment, that there was a serial killer on the loose, where were the police to look? There was, it seemed, an embarrassment of suspects – dozens of violent Johns who had been rounded up on assault charges during the previous two decades.

However, Robert Pickton was not among them. Should he have been?

In 1997, Pickton got into a knife fight with a prostitute on his farm that resulted in both being treated in the same hospital.

Nurses removed a handcuff from around the woman's wrist using a key that was on Pickton's person. He was charged with attempted murder, though this was later dismissed.

In 1998, Bill Hiscox, one of Pickton's employees, approached police to report on a supposed charity, the Piggy Palace Good Times Society, that was run by Robert and his brother Daniel. Housed in a converted building on the pig farm, Hiscox claimed that it was nothing but a party place populated by a rotating cast of prostitutes.

It wasn't the first police had heard of the Piggy Palace Good Times Society. Established in 1996 to 'co-ordinate, manage and operate special events, functions, dances, shows and exhibitions on behalf of service organizations, sports organizations and other worthy groups', it had continually violated Port Coquitlam city bylaws. There were parties – so many parties – drawing well over 1,000 people to a property that was zoned as agricultural.

The strange goings-on at the Piggy Palace Good Times Society might have been a concern, but Hiscox's real focus had to do with the missing women. The Pickton employee told police that purses and other items that could identify the prostitutes would be found on the pig farm.

Police visited the Port Coquitlam property on at least four occasions, once with Hiscox in tow, but found nothing. Robert Pickton would become nothing more than one of many described as 'a person of interest'.

The years passed, women kept disappearing, and still the notion of a serial killer at work in the Downtown Eastside was dismissed.

By 2001, the number of women who had gone missing from the neighbourhood had grown to 65 – a number that police could no longer ignore. That April, a team called 'The Missing Women Task Force' was established. The arrest of Gary Ridgway seven months later by American authorities brought fleeting interest. Better known as the 'Green River Killer', Ridgway killed scores of prostitutes in the Seattle area, roughly 240 km (150 miles) south of Vancouver. The many murders coincided with the disappearances of the missing women, but it quickly became clear that Ridgway had had nothing to do with events north of the border. The Missing Women Task Force looked into other American serial killers, as well, including foot fetishist Dayton Rogers, 'The Malolla Forest Killer', who had murdered several prostitutes in Oregon.

Despite the newly established task force, prostitutes continued to disappear. No one foresaw the events of February 2002.

Early in the month, Pickton was arrested, imprisoned and charged with a variety of firearms offences, including storing a firearm contrary to regulations, possession of a firearm without a licence and possession of a loaded restricted firearm without a licence. In carrying out the search warrant that led to the charges, police uncovered personal possessions belonging to one of the missing women.

Pickton was released on bail, but was kept under surveillance. On 22 February, he was again taken into custody – this time to be charged with two counts of first-degree murder in the deaths of prostitutes Sereena Abotsway and Mona Wilson. The pig farmer would never again experience a day of freedom.

The Pickton farm soon came to look like something out of a science fiction film. Investigators and forensics specialists in contamination suits searched for signs of the missing women. Severed heads were found in a freezer, a wood chipper contained further fragments, and still more were found in a pigpen and in pig feed. These were easy finds; a team of 52 anthropologists were brought in to do the rest, sifting through 14 acres of soil in search of bones, teeth and hair.

Their diligence brought over 10,000 separate pieces of evidence – and, for Pickton, this meant a further 24 counts of murder.

But to the citizens of Vancouver, particularly the friends and families of the missing women, the breakthrough had come far too late. In place of praise came criticism. How was it that the police had found nothing at all suspicious when they'd visited the farm just a few years earlier? Sereena Abotsway, Mona Wilson and several other women whose body parts were found on the farm had disappeared after those initial searches. Might their lives have been spared?

We might add to these questions: What do we now make of Robert Pickton? A decade after he made headlines as Canada's most prolific serial killer, his picture is still coming into focus.

Pickton promised prostitutes not only cash, but drugs and alcohol, if they would only come to Piggy Palace. It's thought that he would almost invariably accuse each of his victims of stealing. He bound each woman, before strangling them with a wire or a belt. Pickton would then drag his victim to the farm's slaughterhouse, where he would use his skills as a butcher.

Some remains he buried on the farm, while others were fed to his pigs. Still more was disposed of at West Coast Reduction Ltd, an 'animal rendering and recycling plant' located well within walking distance of Main and Hastings, the worst corner in the country. In fact, dozens of prostitutes strolled the streets in the shadow of the plant. Eventually, the remains would find their way into cosmetics and animal feed.

Testing found the DNA of some victims in the pork found on the farm. The meat processed on the farm was never sold commercially, though Pickton did distribute it among friends and neighbours.

It took nearly five years and $100 million to prepare the case against Pickton. The pig farmer denied his guilt to all but one person: a police officer who had been posing as a cellmate. The pig farmer's words were caught by a hidden camera: 'I was gonna do one more, make it an even 50. That's why I was sloppy. I wanted one more. Make… make the big five O.'

Pickton seemed to acknowledge that he was stuck, that there was no way he would be found not guilty. 'I think I'm nailed to the cross,' he told the bogus cellmate. 'But if that happens there will be about 15 other people are gonna go down.'

The statement only added to suspicions that the remains found on the pig farm weren't solely Pickton's work. Yet, on 22 January 2007, when the pig farmer finally had his day in court, he went alone.

The trial proceeded on a group of six counts that had been drawn from the 26 that Pickton faced. As explained by Justice James Williams, the severing had taken place in the belief that a trial dealing with all 26 might take as long as two years to complete, and would place too high a burden on the jury.

As it was, Pickton's trial on the six charges lasted nearly 11 months, and was the longest in Canadian history. Pickton, who had pleaded not guilty on all counts, sat barely paying attention as 128 witnesses took the stand.

That he was found guilty came as a surprise to no one. On 9 December 2007, after nine long days of deliberation, jurors found Pickton guilty only of six counts of second-degree murder. The men and women were not convinced that Pickton had acted alone.

Robert Pickton was sentenced to life in prison. Though he will be eligible for parole after 25 years, it is unlikely to be granted.

ANDERS BEHRING BREIVIK

ON THE AFTERNOON of 22 July 2011, a curious compendium titled *2083: A European Declaration of Independence* was emailed to over a thousand recipients around the globe. Its author was a complete unknown, but by the end of the day he would be famous – not for his writing, but as the worst spree killer in world history.

Anders Behring Breivik was born on 13 February 1979 in Oslo, but lived most of his earliest days in London, where his father, an economist, worked as a diplomat for the Royal Norwegian Embassy. At the age of one, his parents divorced, setting off a custody battle that his father lost. Still an infant, Breivik returned with his mother, a nurse, to Oslo. Although she was soon remarried, to a Norwegian Army officer, Breivik would later criticize what he perceived as an absence of the masculine in his childhood home. In his writings, he disparages his mother for his 'matriarchal upbringing', adding 'it completely lacked discipline and has contributed to feminizing me to a certain degree.'

Anecdotal evidence shows Breivik to have been an intelligent, caring boy, one who was quick to defend others against bullying. However, his behaviour changed markedly in adolescence. Over a two-year period, so Breivik claims, he engaged in a one-man 'war' against Oslo's public transit company, causing £700,000 ($956,000) in property damage. His evenings were spent running around the city with friends, committing acts of vandalism.

At 16, Breivik was caught spray-painting graffiti on the exterior wall of a building, an act that brought an end to his relationship with his father. The two have had no contact since.

Though the stepson of an army officer, Breivik was declared 'unfit for service' in Norway's mandatory conscription assessment. The reason for this surprising judgement has yet to be disclosed; Breivik told friends a story that he'd received an exemption to care for his sickly mother. However, a possible explanation is his use of anabolic steroids, a drug that he'd been taking since his teenage years in an effort to bulk up. Breivik was a man obsessed with his appearance.

A picture of Anders Behring Breivik from his personal website.

In 2000, at the age of 21, he flew to the USA to have cosmetic surgery on his forehead, nose and chin. Unmarried at 32, Breivik considered himself a most desirable bachelor, and boasted frequently of his conquests, yet not one of his acquaintances can remember him ever having a girlfriend.

'When it comes to girls,' Breivik wrote in his journal, 'I'm tempted – especially these days, after training and I'm feeling fantastic. But I try to avoid entanglements, because they may complicate my plans and put the whole operation in jeopardy.'

The operation he referred to was part of a nine-year plan that culminated on that horrible day in July 2011. According to Breivik, work began in 2002 with the establishment of a computer programming business that was intended to raise funds. Instead, the company went bankrupt, forcing him to move back to his mother's house. This humiliating setback seems to have brought on a period of relative inactivity. By 2009, however, Breivik was back in business. He set up a company, Breivik Geofarm, which was nothing more than a cover so that he might buy large quantities of fertilizer and other chemicals used in bomb-making without raising suspicions. The next year, after a failed attempt at buying illegal weapons in Prague, he purchased a semi-automatic Glock pistol and a Ruger Mini-14 semi-automatic carbine through legal channels.

Breivik murdered with these guns, but his first victims on 22 July 2011 were killed with a car bomb planted in his Volkswagen Crafter. That afternoon, he drove the automobile into the government quarter of Oslo, taking care to park it in front of the building housing the Office of the Prime Minister, the Minister of Justice and Police and several other high-ranking government ministers. At 3:22 pm, the car bomb exploded, shattering windows, and setting the ground floor of the building on fire. Though Labour Prime Minister Jens Stoltenberg, thought to have been a chief target of the attack, survived without a scratch, the explosion killed eight people and left 11 more with critical injuries.

Things could have been much worse. It's curious that through all Breivik's years of planning, he'd never taken into account the fact that July is the month Norwegians go on holiday. What's more, he'd chosen to carry out his attack late on a Friday afternoon, a time when most government employees had already left for the weekend.

During the mayhem in downtown Oslo, Breivik changed into a fake police uniform, made his way some 40 km (25 miles) to the shores of Lake

Tyrifjorden, and caught a ferry to the island of Utoya. His destination was a summer camp that was held annually by the youth wing of the Norwegian Labour Party. By the time he arrived – 4:45 pm, one hour and 23 minutes after the Oslo blast – news of the tragedy had already been announced to the camp staff and roughly 600 teenagers on the island. Breivik appeared as he presented himself: a police officer who had come to ensure that the 26-acre island was secure. After first asking people to gather around so that he could speak with them, Breivik opened fire. He shot indiscriminately, apparently intent on killing as many people as possible. Breivik's bullets even struck people as they took to the lake, hoping to swim to safety.

It wasn't until 32 minutes after the shooting began that police on the mainland were aware of something taking place on Utoya Island. Their delayed response became a matter for investigation. They waited until the Beredskapstroppen, a special counter-terrorism unit, arrived from Oslo, before making the crossing. The boat that they sailed on was so overloaded that it nearly sank before reaching the island. Even before they left shore, Breivik placed a phone call to surrender, only to change his mind. The killing continued until 6:26 pm – one hour and 24 minutes after it had begun – when the gunman made a second call. He was apprehended by the Beredskapstroppen eight minutes later.

In all, Breivik killed 69 people on Utoya Island and its surrounding waters. Many of the survivors escaped with their lives by swimming to areas that were only accessible from the lake, while others hid in a schoolhouse, which the gunman chose not to enter. Some survivors played dead, even after being shot for a second time. Still others were rescued by vacationers and by those with boats, who risked coming under fire from the shore.

Breivik claimed a total of 77 lives with his two attacks; a further 153 people were injured. The dead ranged in age from 14 to 61, with a median age of just 18 years. He'd killed 55 teenagers.

Anders Breivik has acknowledged that he committed the bombing in Oslo and the shootings on Utoya, but has denied guilt. In his words, both events involved 'atrocious but necessary actions'. These four words came from his lawyer. Much of the gunman's motivation can be gleaned through *2083: A European Declaration of Independence*, the 1,513-page document that he released to the world just 90 minutes before setting off the Oslo bomb. In this collection of writings, much of it plagiarized from others, Breivik argues against feminism and for a return to a patriarchy that he felt was lacking in his own upbringing. The murderer rails against multiculturalism and what he sees as opening the door to the Islamization of Europe. Portraying himself as a knight, Breivik calls on other white Europeans to wage a religious war against Muslims and Marxists. His ultimate goal, as reflected in the title of the document, was the deportation of all followers of Islam from Europe by 2083.

'A majority of the people I know support my views,' he writes, 'they are just apathetic. They know that there will be a confrontation one day, but they don't care because it will most likely not happen within the next two decades.'

In court Breivik alluded to himself as the future regent of Norway. He said one of his tasks would be to carry out executions of 'category A, B and C traitors,' while enlisting selected Norwegians for breeding purposes on special reservations. In 2012, he was given a sentence known as containment, which under Norwegian law specifies a period of imprisonment not less than ten years but with no upper limit, meaning that Anders Breivik can, and probably will, be imprisoned for the rest of his life.

UNITED STATES
OF AMERICA

ALBERTO ANASTASIA

IN 1957, NOTHING became Alberto Anastasia's life so much as his leaving of it. For he lived by violence – and he died by it. The boss of Murder Incorporated, New York's so-called 'Lord High Executioner,' was ultimately executed by those he'd once served. He had, to use a later expression, by then passed his sell-by date. The days of the gun-toting street-fighter were over.

Alberto Anastasia seems to have arrived in New York from Sicily as an illegal immigrant during the First World War. But he was soon cutting his criminal teeth – like so many other future Mafia leaders – in the gang of Jacob 'Little Augie' Orgen, a New York labour-union racketeer. Orgen's assassination in 1927 split the gang into factions, and Anastasia soon threw in his lot with the three men who were to reshape and reorganize the Mafia on a national basis: Meyer Lansky, Vito Genovese and 'Lucky' Luciano. He became one of their strong-arms and hit-men, alongside 'Bugsy' Siegel; when the New York Commission – or National Crime Syndicate – was finally set up, he became the founding father of its enforcement arm, taking responsibility for long-distance contract killings.

In 1940, though, Abe Reles, one of Anastasia's killers-for-hire, turned stoolie and started giving detailed evidence about dozens of murders in which Anastasia was implicated. He went underground and only re-emerged in November 1941 when Reles had an unfortunate 'accident,' falling six floors to his death from the hotel in which the Brooklyn District Attorney had hidden him, under supposed police protection.

No one was ever charged in Reles's death. But the case against Anastasia, with him out of the way, collapsed; and he was free to play his part, after the war and the exile of 'Lucky' Luciano to Italy, in the vicious mob battles for control of Luciano's gambling, prostitution and drugs operations in the US. He emerged as head of the Mangano family. But his style of doing business – and his increasing ambition – didn't sit well with the bosses of the other clans. So on 25 October 1957, when Anastasia went down to the basement barber's shop in Manhattan's Park-Sheraton Hotel for his regular haircut, two men followed him and shot him to death with automatic pistols as he sat in the barber's chair. Then they threw down their weapons, went back up to street-level and disappeared.

Ten years later, a Mafia soldier called Joe Valachi claimed that the killing had been ordered by Anastasia's old associate, Vito Genovese, on the grounds that Anastasia had been invading his turf. The members of the Commission had agreed. In the old days, of course, at this point they would have got in touch with Murder Incorporated – and Alberto Anastasia himself.

JOE BALL

JOE BALL WAS a large man, over six feet tall, with a big appetite and lots of muscle. He was also an expert with guns; he kept alligators – and he scared people. He scared the ranch owner next to his hooch house in Elmendorf, Texas, so badly that he moved his family to California even before he sold up. His third wife took off in the same direction and for the same reason, and when a neighbour came calling one day to complain about a foul smell from a rain barrel near the alligator pool, he learned never to complain again. Even the cops weren't immune. When one of them asked in passing why so many of the waitresses at Ball's saloon, The Sociable Club, seemed just to stay for a while and then vanish, he got a gun in his face and a death-threat for his pains – and not even he took it any further.

Ball was born a rich kid in 1894 – his family had cattle and were big in business. But, after spending time at the University of Texas, he just didn't seem interested in anything his parents had to offer. Instead he went to the bad and made a small fortune of his own as a bootlegger, doing most of his business from bed. His clients said that he didn't even bother to look up much as he busied himself with whichever young girl was currently occupying it. Just so long as he got his money.

In the late 1920s, with Prohibition on the wane, Ball opened The Sociable Club and the stream of young women coming through his door and into his bed kept on flowing: this time waitresses and barkeepers. Sometimes he married them, sometimes he didn't; but his reputation as a good ol' boy kept spreading. He bought himself five alligators, which he kept in a cement pool behind the club; he took favoured customers out there to watch him toss them fresh meat, just to see them thrashing. He also had a pen by the pool which he filled with live stray dogs and cats. The very privileged were allowed to see the fun as he tossed them in too.

Then in 1938, the relatives of one of his waitresses, 22-year-old Hazel Brown, told local police that she'd disappeared. She'd previously been seen around town with Ball; they were obviously lovers. But no one had seen her leave Elmendorf and none of the money in a bank account she'd opened had been withdrawn. So on 24 September Texas Ranger Lee Miller went out to see Ball, and as a precaution took some other law-enforcement people with him.

Ball seemed unfazed at first by their arrival and by the questions they asked. But then he went behind the bar, took a revolver out of the cash register and, as he stood in front of the cops, blew off the top of his own head. His terrified handyman was then interviewed at length, and led them to the remains of Hazel Brown in the rain barrel. There were still traces of blood in the alligator pool.

The handyman later admitted that Ball had killed many young women, including two of his wives, one of whom he'd seen chopped up and fed to the alligators. Then came more witnesses: his third wife, found in California, admitted she too had witnessed a murder; the ranch owner from next door said he'd come across Ball cutting up another woman's body and feeding it to the 'gators. Both had fled for their lives.

Ball seems to have killed up to 20 young women, most of whom he'd made pregnant. They were disposed of simply because they became a nuisance with their constant nagging about marriage. The handyman, Clifford Wheeler – who also claimed to have been terrified of Ball – was sentenced to four years as an accessory to murder. And the alligators? They were sent to a zoo in San Antonio, where they entertained visitors for many years...

MA BARKER

MA BARKER AND her boys were a crime wave on the hoof, a close-knit and mobile Murder Incorporated. With their chief partner-in-crime Alvin Karpis, they executed anyone who was suspected of betraying them or selling them short; they did mail-robberies, held up banks, organized kidnaps, and shot down anyone in uniform who happened to cross their path, including, on one occasion, employees of Northwest Airways. There's no evidence that Ma herself had ever committed much in the way of crime before 1932 when the gang first hit the headlines. But with her sons along, she was a fast learner.

She was born Arizona Donnie Clark in the Ozarks, the wild mountainous backwoods of Missouri, of Scots, Irish and Indian blood; and all her sons, one way and another, went to the bad. By the beginning of the '30s, 'Doc' was in the Oklahoma State Pen for killing a nightwatchman; Hermann was doing 25 years in Leavenworth for mail-robbery; and Fred was just coming to the end of a stint digging coal in the State Penitentiary in Kansas, where he'd become friends with a killer called Alvin Karpis.

It was Fred and Alvin Karpis, when they came out of jail together, who first set the ball rolling. A few days after a robbery, they killed a sheriff who was inspecting the De Soto they'd used for it. So they took it on the lam from Ma's shack in Thayer, Missouri, to a furnished house in St. Paul, taking Ma and her live-in lover, Arthur Dunlop, with them. Dunlop, though, wasn't to last long. For after living quietly for a while, they narrowly escaped a police raid on their new headquarters. They must have decided that it was Dunlop who'd betrayed them. For a day later his naked, bullet-riddled body was found by a lake near Webster, Wisconsin. There was a blood-stained woman's glove beside it.

From now on Ma seems only to have trusted ex-cons and escapers from one or other of her three boys' jails. Several of these now joined Fred, Alvin Karpis and her; when the growing gang took a bank in Fort Scott, Kansas, in June 1932, they used the proceeds to stage a welcome home party for one of Fred's ex-cellmates. Three months later, with some of the $240,000 that they heisted from the Cloud County Bank in Concordia, Kansas, they bought 'Doc's' parole from the Oklahoma Pen – and even 'two years of absence' for his partner-in crime, Volney Davis. Leavenworth, though, proved a more difficult proposition. Hermann stayed behind bars.

December 1932: Minneapolis, Third Northwestern Bank – two policeman and a civilian killed. April 1933: Fairbury, Nebraska, Fairbury National Bank – one gang member killed. June 1933: Minneapolis, Arthur Hamm Jr, of the Hamm Brewing Company kidnapped – yield, $100,000. The kidnappings, the bank-heists and the killings went on through 1933. In South St. Paul, one policeman was killed, another crippled for life. In Chicago, a traffic cop was gunned down while enquiring about an accident with the gang's car, unaware that bank messengers had been recently held up nearby. The pressure on Ma's boys and the offers of rewards, though, began to pile up; and it was because of this, perhaps, that they decided in January 1934 to go for the big one.

They'd first decided simply to rob the Commercial State Bank in St. Paul. Then they decided to kidnap the bank's president. After a month's negotiations about the ransom and conditions, they took the enormous sum of $200,000 – enough, they thought, to buy them new identities and new lives. Fred and 'Doc' Barker, Alvin Karpis and a few of the others had their fingerprints shaved off and their faces surgically altered. And then they all scattered to locations across the United States, from Montana to Florida, Nevada, Ohio and elsewhere.

A year after the kidnapping, for all this, 'Doc' was picked up in the apartment of his Chicago girlfriend and in it was found a map of Florida, with the area around Ocala and Lake Weir circled. This coincided with a tip the Feds had had: that Ma and Fred were hiding somewhere in the south, where there was a famous alligator known to locals as 'Old Joe'. Within days, then, they raided a cottage on the shore of Lake Weir. Ma and Fred put up a fight, but by the time the shooting was over, they were both dead, Ma with a machine gun still in her hand. There were enough weapons in the cottage, J. Edgar Hoover later said,

'to keep a regiment at bay.'

The rest of the gang were soon picked up, in ones and twos, in Toledo, Ohio, and Allandale, Florida; and finally Alvin Karpis was run to ground in New Orleans. Years later, after being sentenced to life imprisonment, Karpis, whose real name was Francis Albin Karpavicz, taught Charlie Manson the guitar.

DAVID BERKOWITZ

ON 17 APRIL 1977, a letter was found on a Bronx street in New York from a postal worker called David Berkowitz. It was addressed to a police captain and read in part:

'I am deeply hurt by your calling me a woman-hater. I am not. But I am a monster… I am a little brat… I am the Son of Sam.'

Nearby was a parked car in which Berkowitz's latest victims, a young courting couple, had been arbitrarily gunned down. Valentina Suriani had died immediately; Alexander Esau died later in hospital, with three bullets in his head.

No one, of course, knew then that the 'Son of Sam' was the pudgy 24-year-old Berkowitz. But for nine months he'd been terrorizing the late-night streets of Queens and the Bronx. He'd killed three people and wounded four, seemingly without any motive at all. New York City Mayor Abe Beame had held a press conference to announce: 'We have a savage killer on the loose.'

The first attack had come out of the blue on 29 July 1976 at about one o'clock in the morning, when two young women, one a medical technician, the other a student nurse, were sitting chatting in the front seats of an Oldsmobile parked on a Bronx street. A man had walked up to them, pulled a gun out of a paper bag and fired five shots, killing one of them and wounding the other in the thigh. Four months later, the same gun had been used, again after midnight, against two girls sitting outside a house in Queens. A man had walked up to them and asked directions; then he'd

The 'Son of Sam' terrified New Yorkers.

simply opened fire. Both young women had been badly wounded, and one of them, with a bullet lodged in her spine, paralysed.

In between these two shootings, there had been yet another one – it turned out later from forensic evidence – using the same .44. Another young couple had been sitting in front of a tavern – again at night and once more in Queens – when someone had fired shots through the back window. The man had been rushed to hospital, but had recovered; the woman had not been hit.

The panic really began, though, with the mysterious killer's fourth and fifth attacks. On 8 March 1977, a young Armenian student, Virginia Voskerichian, was shot in the face at close range only a few hundred yards from her home in Queens, and instantly killed. Forty days later, with the deaths of Valentina Suriani and Alexander Esau and the discovery of the letter, it became clear that the killings weren't going to stop. More than that, the killer now had a name – and it was a name to stir up nightmares.

'I love to hunt. Prowling the streets, looking for fair game – tasty
    meat,'

wrote the 'Son of Sam'.

Restaurants, bars and discos in Queens and the Bronx were by now closing early for lack of business. People stayed home and kept off the streets at night, despite the deployment of 100 extra patrolmen and the setting-up of a special squad of detectives. For no one had any idea when 'the Son of Sam' might strike again, and the nearest description the police had been able to come up with was that he was a 'neurotic, schizophrenic and paranoid' male, who probably believed himself possessed by demons...

He could, from that description, be any man at all – that was what was so frightening. He could even be a policeman himself – which might explain why he'd proved so elusive. This idea began to take hold when he struck yet again in the early hours of a late-June morning, shooting through the windscreen of a car in Queens and wounding another young couple. All the police could do in response to the gathering panic was once more to beef up foot patrols in anticipation of the anniversary of his first murder a year before.

Nothing happened, though, on the night of 29 July 1977; and when he did strike again, it wasn't in his usual hunting-ground at all – but in Brooklyn. In the early hours of 31 July, he fired through the windshield at a pair of young lovers sitting in their car near the sea-front at Coney Island. The woman died in hospital; the man recovered, but was blinded.

This time, though, the 'Son of Sam' had made a mistake. For a woman out walking her dog at about the same time not far away saw two policemen ticketing a car parked near a fire hydrant and then, a few minutes later, a young man jumping into the car and driving off. As it happened only one car, a Ford Galaxie, was ticketed that night for parking at a hydrant – and it was registered to a David Berkowitz in Yonkers.

When approached the next day by the police officer in charge of the search, Berkowitz instantly recognized him from the TV, and said,

'Inspector Dowd? You finally got me.'

As a figure of nightmare, Berkowitz was something of a let-down: an overweight loner with a moronic smile who lived in squalor, was pathologically shy of women and probably still a virgin. He later said he heard demons urging him to kill, among them a 6,000-year-old man who had taken over the body of a dog he had shot. On the walls of his apartment he'd scrawled a series of demonic slogans:

'In this hole lives the wicked king'; 'Kill for my Master'; and 'I turn children into killers'.

Berkowitz was judged sane, and was sentenced to a total of 365 years in prison. His apartment became a place of pilgrimage for a ghoulish fan-club; and he himself has since made a great deal of money from articles, a book and the film rights to his life.

KENNETH BIANCHI AND ANGELO BUONO

KENNETH BIANCHI AND Angelo Buono were cousins – and in their way opposites. Still, they made a good team. For Buono was all macho, a street-tough, hanging out with hookers and forever parading his Italian connections, while Bianchi was a lot more subtle and plausible. He read books on psychology, applied to join the LA Police, and even rode in patrol cars with cops who – though they didn't know it – were out there looking for him. He was also, no doubt, keeping an eye at the time on exactly how the cops approached people on the street. For it was almost certainly Bianchi who persuaded the women they killed that he and his cousin were undercover cops – and sweet-talked them into their car.

Bianchi, who'd been raised by foster parents in the east, arrived in Glendale, California, in 1977, to stay with cousin Buono, who ran an upholstery business out of his garage. In October of that year the first victim of a killer who came to be called the 'Hillside Strangler' was found near Chevy Chase Drive; and within two weeks there was another, this time dumped among the gravestones of Forest Lawn Cemetery. Both women were naked, and the body of the second had been carefully washed – apart from the marks of ropes tied round her wrists, ankles and neck, there were no clues at all.

By the middle of December, seven more bodies had been found, all women and young girls between the ages of 12 and 28. Most, though not all, had been part-time prostitutes. They were naked and most had been tied up, raped and sodomized before they'd been strangled and then carefully washed. All of them had been dumped in places where they could be easily found, often close to police precinct-houses – as if the 'Strangler' were making fun of the cops' inability to find him.

There was one more killing, in February 1978, when the body of yet another young woman was found, this time in the trunk of a car. But then they stopped. It was only much later that the police discovered that all ten bodies had been placed in a rough circle round Angelo Buono's house.

They discovered it because almost a year later, in January 1979, Bianchi, who'd moved to Bellingham, Washington, because of the mess in Buono's house, raped and strangled two co-eds and made the mistake of shoving their bodies into the trunk of one of the co-eds' car. They were found relatively quickly, and Bianchi had been seen with one of them. He was brought in for questioning.

Bianchi played a game with the police – he was working as a security guard and had made another application to join the force in Bellingham. At first he was charm itself and denied everything. But then little by little he began to drop hints about the existence of several Kenneth Bianchis inside him, one of whom might have committed the murders. He had black-outs, he said; he couldn't remember things he'd done; perhaps a secret interior murderer had done them.

In the end he was charged with the murder of the two Bellingham students; at this point he calmly offered a deal. He would plead guilty, he said, and finger his Californian cousin as the real 'Hillside Strangler,' if he could avoid the death penalty in Washington and serve time in a California prison instead. The authorities agreed, and he was sentenced to life imprisonment.

Once Bianchi had been shipped to California, though, it turned out there was a problem – one which Bianchi himself may well have anticipated. For, guilty or not, he'd fooled Washington psychiatrists into declaring him insane – and as such, of course, he couldn't give evidence against Buono. It later transpired that he'd made a close study of Sybil and The Three Faces of Eve, books about multiple personalities; and had almost certainly duped psychiatrists into believing he'd been successfully hypnotized when revealing details about his own.

Buono did in the end come to trial. But, without Bianchi, it was a long and extremely difficult case, since Buono, before his arrest, had cleared his apartment of every trace of evidence except for a single eyelash that belonged to one of their victims. In the end his conviction probably hinged on the evidence of a woman who identified him and Bianchi as the two 'detectives' who'd stopped her on a Hollywood street and demanded to see her ID. She was the daughter of the actor Peter Lorre, and Bianchi later admitted that he'd seen a picture of her father next to the ID in her wallet and had decided to let her go.

After two years of trial and more than 400 witnesses, Buono was finally sentenced to life without possibility of parole, and died of a heart attack in his prison cell in 2002. Bianchi was ordered back to Walla Walla Prison in Washington, and will not be eligible for parole until 2025.

BILLY THE KID

BILLY THE KID, later to become one of the great legends of the West, was born Henry McCarty in a slum tenement in New York on 23 November 1859. At the age of three, he moved with his parents to Caffeyville, Kansas, where his father died. His mother soon moved on, this time to Colorado, and married a miner and prospector who took them to the raw boom town of Silver City, New Mexico, where his mother opened a boarding-house.

His mother died when Billy was 14 or 15; and soon afterwards, on the run from a charge of petty theft in New Mexico, he killed a bully in

Arizona. From then on he took the name of William Bonney; and back in New Mexico, became a cowboy working on the ranch of an Englishman called John Henry Tunstall.

Tunstall, along with cattle baron John Chisum, had decided to take on the power of a group of crooked rancher-businessmen called 'The House' who had turned Lincoln County into their own political and economic fiefdom. He was assassinated by The House on 17 February 1878. But his gun-carrying cowhands, led by teenage Billy, stayed loyal to his cause; and what became known as the Lincoln County War raged through the territory for the next four months, culminating in a five-day-long battle in the single street of Lincoln, New Mexico, in July. Tunstall's men were eventually routed, with many killed, but Billy made the first of what was to become a series of legendary escapes.

At this point he did his best to become a law-abiding citizen. But New Mexico governor Lew Wallace – who later wrote the best-selling novel *Ben Hur* – reneged on a deal he'd made offering Billy a pardon in return for his testimony against two vicious killers; and John Chisum, who was notoriously mean, refused him the back-pay he'd earned for his part in the war, perhaps because of Billy's liaison with his niece.

Billy had no alternative, then, but to become a full-time cowboy outlaw. With other veterans of the war he took to rustling in Lincoln County and beyond. This soon brought down on him the forces of big-money: a new alliance of town businessmen, cattlemen and professionals, mostly from White Oaks and Roswell. Billy, however, was liked by, and had wide support from, ordinary townspeople and smallholders; and when his onetime friend Pat Garrett, a former buffalo hunter, was put up as sheriff of Lincoln, he backed another nominee to run against him.

The rest, as they say, is history. Pat Garrett won, broke up the gang and arrested Billy, who was tried and condemned for homicide during the Lincoln County War. With no pardon available from the Governor, he killed two guards and escaped. By now made famous by newspapers and dime-store novels, he was tracked down by Garrett and a range-detective called John Poe to Fort Sumner on the Pecos River; and gunned down at night there by a single bullet from Garrett's gun.

It's not quite history, of course. For a year after his death, an itinerant newsman called Ash Upson wrote a 25 cent pamphlet for Pat Garrett called *Saga of Billy the Kid* and years later he ghosted another work for Garrett, *The*

Authentic Life of Billy the Kid. In both books, the literate and likeable Billy was transmuted into a psychopath: a deadly shot and a multiple murderer, all for the greater glory of Garrett and the so-called forces of law and order. When he was killed, Billy the Kid was 21.

LIZZIE BORDEN

LIZZIE BORDEN, SO the old rhyme goes, took an axe and gave her mother 40 whacks; when she saw what she had done, she gave her father 41. The truth is, though, that the number of whacks which despatched Abbey Borden and her rich husband Andrew in Fall River, Massachusetts, in 1892, numbered 19 and ten respectively – and daughter Lizzie, much to the delight of the courtroom which tried her, was finally acquitted.

But was she really guilty? She certainly had a motive. For Abbey was in fact 32-year-old Lizzie's stepmother, and she resented her deeply, particularly after her father, usually very tight with his money, bought Abbey's sister a house and gave the deeds to his wife. Lizzie was also given to what her family had come to call 'funny turns'. One day, for example, she announced to her father that Abbey's bedroom had been ransacked by a burglar. He reported it to the police, who soon established that Lizzie had done the ransacking herself.

As for her father, whom she loved, the repressed spinster may even have had a motive for his murder too, apart from his meanness with money and the fact that, with both him and her stepmother dead, she would finally inherit it. For three months before his death in August, when outhouses in the garden were twice broken into, he'd convinced himself that whoever was responsible had been after Lizzie's pet pigeons. So he'd decapitated them – yes, with an axe.

Suffice it to say that at about 9:30 am on 4 August, while dusting the spare room, Abbey Borden was struck from behind with an axe and then brutally hacked at even after she was dead. There were only two people in the house at the time, Lizzie and the maid Bridget who was cleaning the downstairs windows. Slightly less than an hour and a half later, Andrew Borden returned, to be told by his daughter that his wife was out. A few minutes later, after Bridget had gone upstairs to her room in the attic, he too was struck down while dozing on a settee in the living-room.

It was Lizzie who 'found' the body of her father, and the neighbours she immediately called in found the body of his wife upstairs. They did their best to comfort her. But she seemed curiously calm, and she was happy enough to talk to the police as soon as they arrived. Trouble was that, both then and subsequently, she began giving conflicting accounts of her whereabouts during the morning; and it wasn't long before the police, who found a recently cleaned axehead in the basement, came to regard her as the chief suspect. Only the day before the murders she'd tried to buy prussic acid in Fall River, they discovered, and when that had failed, she'd told a neighbour she was worried that her father had made many potentially vengeful enemies, because of his brusque manner.

After the inquest she was arrested – and vilified as a murderess in the newspapers. But by the time her trial took place in New Bedford in 1893, the tide had begun to turn. Bridget and her sister played down her hatred of her stepmother; and though Bridget confessed that Lizzie had burned one of her dresses on the day after her parents' funeral, she said that there had been no bloodstains on it. Lizzie herself was demure and ladylike in the dock – she even fainted halfway through the proceedings. And in the end the jury agreed with her lawyer, an ex-governor of the State, that she could not be both a lady and a fiend.

After the trial, now rich, she returned to Fall River and bought a large house, in which she died alone in 1927. Bridget the maid returned to Ireland – with, it's said, a good deal of money from poor Andrew Borden's coffers. There's since been a suggestion that Lizzie became a killer during one of her 'funny turns' – caused by temporal-lobe epilepsy.

JERRY BRUDOS

JERRY BRUDOS, 30 years old, was a Portland, Oregon, electrician and amateur photographer, married, with two children. He was quietly-spoken and apparently gentle; and he spent the evening with his co-ed date talking quietly to her in the lounge of her college dormitory. But somewhere nearby there was a serial killer on the loose and when he said to her that she 'ought to feel sad' for the girls who'd been killed, she thought it sufficiently odd to mention it to the police. It didn't mean much, she agreed, and she nearly didn't. But if she hadn't, then the police

– and Brudos's wife – might never have found out what he got up to in the studio in his basement garage.

In 1968, three young Oregon women vanished into thin air and it wasn't until March 1969 that one of them – her body too decomposed for the cause of death to be established – was washed up in a creek. Within a month, two more women had disappeared. But this time they were found relatively quickly, floating in the Long Tom River. Both had been raped and strangled, stripped of bra and panties and weighed down by bits of metal from a car.

There were no clues at all to the identity of the killer. But the police had begun to think that he might just possibly be a transvestite. For in April, a 15-year-old schoolgirl had fought off an attack by a man who tried to force her into his car and two other girls had seen a suspicious man dressed up as a woman in a car park nearby.

It was at this point that the police received the tip-off from the Oregon State co-ed and followed the small thread of her lead back to electrician Jerry Brudos, who turned out, from their records, to be a very strange man indeed. For he'd been arrested for stealing women's underwear and for trying to force a young girl at knifepoint to take off her clothes. He'd been caught near the State University women's dormitory, carrying stolen underwear and wearing a bra and panties.

It was enough for them to search Brudos's house, where they quickly found samples of the type of knots and wire used to tie the weights to the bodies found in the Long Tom River. But this was nothing to what they found in the garage: a souvenir picture of a dead woman hanging from a hook there, with Brudos's face caught reflected in a mirror beneath.

Brudos was arrested and soon confessed to four murders, as well as an obsession with women's underwear and high-heeled shoes. His first victim had been a young door-to-door saleswoman, whom he'd taken to his studio, raped and strangled. Then he'd taken her clothes off and used her as a dummy, fitting her with different bras, panties and shoes from his collection. Finally he'd cut off her left foot, slipped it into a stiletto and stored it in a locked freezer. The rest of her he threw into the Willamette River.

He'd done more or less the same with his next three victims, except that he'd photographed one of them during the fitting-session. He'd also cut off one breast of his second victim, and both breasts of the third. The fourth he had given electric shocks to, just to see if her dead body would twitch.

Brudos was charged with three of these four murders, and pleaded guilty. He was sentenced to three terms of life imprisonment.

TED BUNDY

EVERYONE LIKED THEODORE Bundy. Even the judge at his Miami trial in July 1979 took to him. After sentencing Bundy to death, he said:

'Take care of yourself, young man. I say that to you sincerely. It's a tragedy to this court to see such a total waste of humanity. You're a bright young man. You'd have made a good lawyer. . .'

But Bundy's good looks and intelligence were murderous. For between January 1974 and January 1978, when he was finally arrested in Pensacola, Florida, he brutalized and killed perhaps as many as 36 girls and young women in four states.

The first of these states was Washington, where the disappearances began in the Seattle area at the beginning of 1974. One after another, within six months, seven young women vanished, seemingly into thin air. One of them had been abducted from a rented room; another had left a bar with a man at two in the morning. But the others had simply been out for a walk or on their way somewhere: a cinema or a concert or home. Except for bloodstains in the rented room, they left no trace at all.

In the summer of that year, there were more disappearances, including two in one day from a Washington lakeside resort. But there were also, for the first time, clues. For a good-looking young man with his arm in a sling – and introducing himself as Ted – had been going around the resort asking young women if they could help him load a sailboat onto the roof of his car – and one of the disappeared had been seen going off with him. The scattered remains of both women – and of yet another unknown victim – were found by hunters a few miles away two months later.

A massive manhunt began, producing huge numbers of calls from the public and more than 2,000 potential suspects – among them, thanks to a woman's call, Theodore (Ted) Bundy. But by that time he'd moved to Salt Lake City in Utah to study law; it was there that the disappearances resumed. There were three in October 1974; one the teenage daughter

Bundy always protested his innocence, right up to his execution.

of a local police chief, who was later found – raped, strangled and buried – in the Wassatch Mountains. Then, at the beginning of November, one of his Salt Lake City victims – whom 'a good-looking man' posing as a police officer had lured into his car and had then attacked with a crowbar – managed to escape and to give a description to the police.

Bundy was lucky this time for she failed to recognize him in a photograph the police later showed her. But after one last abduction and murder in Salt Lake City, he from then on began to operate only out-of-state, over the border in Colorado. Between January and July, five more young women disappeared, though this time two of the bodies were discovered quickly. One, with her jeans pulled down, had been beaten to death with a rock. The other had been raped and then bludgeoned.

Bundy, in the end, was picked up by accident, as a possible burglary suspect. But police at the scene found a crowbar, an ice-pick and a ski-mask in his trunk; and in his apartment, maps and brochures of Colorado.

Hairs from the interior of the car were found to match those of the police-chief's dead daughter. He was extradited to Colorado to stand trial, but then he escaped – twice.

The first time he was quickly found hiding out in the mountains. But the second time it took police more than 40 days to catch him, and by then – this time in Florida – another three young women were dead, one of them with teeth marks on her body; three others had been savagely beaten.

The subsequent trial did little to uncover Bundy's reasons for killing – for the sheer viciousness and voracity of his sexual attacks. But in an interview with a detective after his arrest, he remarked,

'Sometimes I feel like a vampire,'

and later, on Death Row, though never confessing to the murders, he speculated to two writers about an early career as a Peeping Tom and a massive consumer of pornography. He also talked about an 'entity' inside him that drove him to rape and murder…

It was the marks of his teeth – so experts confirmed – on a Tallahassee student's body that finally undid Bundy. After numerous, lengthy appeals, he was electrocuted on 24 January 1989, still protesting his innocence.

AL CAPONE

PROHIBITION, WHICH CAME into force in the United States in 1920, was a monumental act of political stupidity. For it was never backed by the ordinary man and woman in the street, and it was they, who by exercising what they saw as their right to go on drinking, handed power to the rum-runners and those who controlled them: men like Al Capone. They voted them, in effect, into office as a sort of underground government. Capone, at his height in the Chicago area, was known as the 'Mayor of Crook County'.

Alfonso Caponi was born in 1899 in New York and grew up into a resourceful small-time hood, working in the rackets and as a bouncer in a Brooklyn brothel – where a knife-fight gave him his nickname: 'Scarface.' In New York, if he'd stayed there, he might never have amounted to much. But in 1920, when on the run from the police, he got an invitation from a distant relative of his family's to join him in Chicago.

The relative was Johnny Torrio, the ambitious chief lieutenant of an old-style Mafia boss called 'Diamond Jim' Colosimo, who controlled most of the brothels in the city. After the passing of the Volstead Act that brought in Prohibition, Torrio had tried to persuade Colosimo to go into the liquor business, but Colosimo'd wanted no part of it. So now Torrio made his move. He despatched Capone, his new personal bodyguard, to Colosimo's restaurant-headquarters one night, and Capone gunned him down.

Torrio, with Capone as his right hand, took over Colosimo's brothels and moved heavily into bootlegging. This brought them into direct competition with the mainly Irish gang of 'Deanie' O'Bannion, a genial ex-choirboy and ex-journalist who served only the finest liquor and ran his business from the city's most fashionable flower-shop. But for a while both sides held their hand. Then in November 1924, in revenge for a trick which got Torrio a police record (and eventually nine months in jail), O'Bannion was killed by three of Torrio's men in his shop, after they'd arrived asking for a funeral wreath.

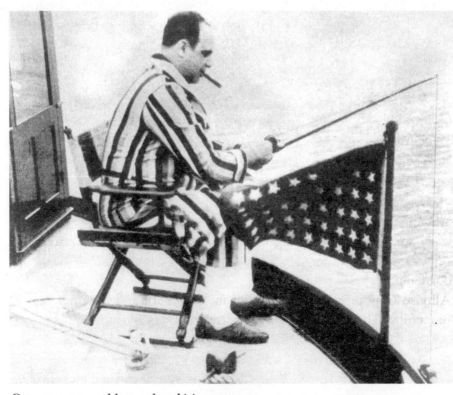

Capone was a ruthless and ambitious gangster.

The death of O'Bannion, who was buried in high style, triggered an all-out war for control of the liquor trade in Chicago, with Torrio and Capone pitted against O'Bannion's lieutenants and heirs, Hymie Weiss and 'Bugs' Moran, and also against the four brothers of the Sicilian Genna family. The going soon got too hot for Johnny Torrio, who in 1925 retired to Naples, taking $50 million, it's said, with him. But Capone was made of sterner – and more cunning – stuff. He gradually eliminated the Genna family and, as he did so, he bought politicians and judges, journalists and police brass, until he was in effect in control, not only of all enforcement agencies and public opinion, but also of City Hall. He made massive donations to the campaigns of Chicago Mayor 'Big Bill' Thompson and he held court to all comers in 50 rooms on two floors of the downtown Metropole Hotel.

In 1929, having already got rid of Hymie Weiss, he was finally ready to move against his last surviving enemy, 'Bugs' Moran. Word was passed to Moran that a consignment of hijacked booze could be picked up at a garage on North Clark Street on St. Valentine's Day, but soon after his people arrived, so did Capone's torpedoes, two of them in police uniform. Six of Moran's men died in what became known as the St. Valentine's Day Massacre, along with an unfortunate optometrist who liked hanging out with hoods; Moran himself only escaped because he was late for the appointment. As for Capone, he was on holiday that day in Biscayne Bay, Florida, and at the actual time of the slaughter at the SMC Cartage Company garage, was on the phone to the Miami DA.

In the end Capone was brought to book, not by the cops, but by the internal revenue service. In 1931, he was tried for tax evasion and sentenced to jail for 11 years. By the time he came out eight years later, the Mafia had moved on, had become more sophisticated; and he himself was not only old hat but half mad from tertiary syphilis. He died in his bed eight years later on his Florida estate. 'Bugs' Moran outlived him by ten years.

BUTCH CASSIDY AND THE SUNDANCE KID

BUTCH CASSIDY, WHOSE parents were both British Mormons, was born George Leroy Parker in Beaver, Utah, in the spring of 1865. As a teenager, he hung out with a cowboy called Mike Cassidy at a ranch his mother was working on; he began calling himself George Cassidy after getting in trouble with the law at 18. A few years later, after joining a cattle-drive, he robbed his first bank at Telluride, Colorado, on 24 June 1889, perhaps in company with a 21-year old Pennsylvanian called Harry Longabaugh – already known to the law as the Sundance Kid.

At the age of about 18, looking for adventure, Longabaugh had travelled with relatives by covered wagon to Colorado; his first nickname-cum-alias had been Kid Chicago. But in 1888, he'd been arrested for rustling near Sundance, Wyoming, and forever after he was known as the Sundance Kid. As for Butch, he seems to have worked briefly as a butcher in Rock Springs between bank- and railroad-heists – and the name stuck.

Butch was a charmer; the Kid, more aloof; both were accomplished escape artists. They each served just one prison stretch, the Kid after the 1888 rustling, and Butch in 1894 for – of all things – stealing a horse. For a while they went their separate ways. The Kid seems to have worked solo. But that was not Butch's way: when he came out of Laramie State Penitentiary after a two-year sentence, he formed a gang which soon became famous as the Wild Bunch. He and a shifting membership, which included Elzy Lay and Harry 'Kid Curry' Logan, went after banks and mine payrolls – and between jobs holed up, first in Robbers' Roost, Utah, and then in the more celebrated Hole-in-the-Wall, Wyoming, a hideaway that had been used by Jesse and Frank James, among others.

It was at Hole-in-the-Wall that Butch and the Kid seem to have joined forces again. In 1899 and 1900, with a series of brilliantly planned hold-ups – beginning with a train robbery at Wilcox, Wyoming which netted between $30,000 and $60,000 – they became both celebrities and very much wanted men. At some point Butch tried to make a deal with both the law and the Union Pacific Railroad – his freedom in return for future good conduct. But when negotiations broke down, the Wild Bunch promptly struck again: they held up another train in Tipton, Wyoming, in August 1900, followed swiftly by a bank hold-up in Winnemucca, Nevada, which yielded another $32,000.

To celebrate, the Bunch went south, to Fort Worth, Texas – and made the big mistake of having a group photograph taken there. For detectives from the Wells Fargo Company and the Pinkerton Agency soon seized on it and had it published both all over the country and as far away, ultimately, as Britain and Tahiti. Bounty hunters pursued them, and to escape the heat, Butch, the Kid and the Kid's lover Etta Place, made their way, first to New York – where the Kid bought Etta a Tiffany watch – and then by steamer to Argentina.

They bought a ranch in Cholilo; Etta and the Kid went back twice to the US on visits. But then they began to run out of money and in March 1906 they started holding up banks again, first in San Luis Province and then in Bahia Blanca. In 1907, they robbed a train in Bolivia and then, swinging back into Argentina, another bank. Etta went back to the States and disappeared, and finally so did Butch and the Kid – either into death or oblivion.

The usual version of the story is that Butch and the Kid were cornered by the military in San Vicente, southern Bolivia, after holding up a mine payroll. There was a furious gun battle; the Kid was fatally wounded and Butch, with his last two bullets, shot, first the Kid, then himself. Butch's sister, though, swore that he paid a visit to his family in Utah in 1925 and that he died 12 years later somewhere in the northwest of the United States. There are also rumours that the Kid joined Etta in Mexico City and died there in 1957. A mining boss, with whom they were friendly, had deliberately misidentified the bodies.

MARK DAVID CHAPMAN

MARK DAVID CHAPMAN wanted to be John Lennon. He collected Beatles records; he'd played in a band; he'd even married an older Japanese woman, just like his hero. But when it finally dawned on him he couldn't be John Lennon, he first attempted suicide, and then he decided that Lennon himself couldn't be John Lennon either.

At the beginning of December 1980, Chapman flew to New York, determined, he said later,

'to go out in a blaze of glory.'

If he couldn't get near John Lennon, he said, he'd shoot himself in the head on top of the Statue of Liberty, because 'no one had killed themselves there before.' But Lennon proved all too accessible. He regularly signed autographs for fans outside his home in the Dakota Building in Manhattan; Chapman joined them there on the morning of 8 December, holding up a copy of Lennon's *Double Fantasy* album for his signature.

He might have left it at that, he later said. But he didn't. For that night, when Lennon and his wife Yoko Ono got back from a recording session, Chapman, who'd waited for hours, calmly walked up to them as they were getting out of their limousine and fired five bullets from a Charter Arms .38 into Lennon's body. Then he simply waited on the sidewalk, holding his signed album and reading a copy of J.D. Salinger's *Catcher in the Rye*, until the police arrived.

At preliminary court hearings and at the eventual trial, the prosecution described the murder as a 'deliberate, premeditated execution,' pointing out that Chapman had not only stalked Lennon before killing him, but also had previous convictions for armed robbery, kidnapping and drugs offences. The defence painted Chapman as someone with an 'incurable disease' who had committed a 'monstrously irrational crime' – he was clearly 'not a sane man.' What neither side seemed to recognize was that in killing John Lennon, Chapman had actually solved the central problem of his life. For he had not only eliminated a role-model it had proved impossible to live up to, he had also made sure that his own name would be from now on inextricably linked to his hero's.

When asked to say something in his defence, Chapman simply read out a passage from *Catcher in the Rye*. He was given a sentence of 20 years to life and recommended for psychiatric treatment. A year later, when visited by a British journalist, he was still reading *Catcher in the Rye*.

CARYL CHESSMAN

CARYL CHESSMAN WAS famous, not for his life, but for his death. When he finally went to the gas chamber in 1960, after 12 years on San Quentin's Death Row, editorials all over Europe denounced his execution as 'appalling' and 'monstrous.' There were violent demonstrations in front of American embassies in Portugal, Ecuador, Uruguay and Venezuela and a cry of condemnation from public figures worldwide. In life, Chessman might have been a violent petty criminal. But in death – and in his preparation for it – his name was amongst the best-known on the planet.

Part of the reason for the outcry was that, so far as was known, Chessman had never killed anyone. Yes, he'd been a criminal from his teens: he'd served time for robbery and escape. But the crimes that had taken him to Death Row were acts of what were called, in the prim language of the times, 'sexual perversion,' forced on two young women he abducted from their cars in the hills above Hollywood in January 1948. The two victims provoked enormous sympathy, of course: one was a married polio sufferer who'd only recently come out of hospital; and the second, a teenager, was later consigned to a mental asylum as irredeemably troubled – she was still there when Chessman was executed.

The evidence, for its part, was more or less watertight. But Chessman had the whole law book thrown at him. He was convicted on 17 charges in all, including two under what was known in California as the 'little Lindbergh Law,' which covered 'kidnapping with intent to rob with bodily harm'. It was these that carried the death penalty.

For 12 years, from 1948 onwards, Chessman literally fought for his life – it became his career. He wrote a novel and three other books about his experiences – one of which, *Cell 2455 Death Row*, became a best-seller. With money from royalties and with the prison library as his basic resource, he launched suit after suit in state and federal courts, attempting to show that he'd been denied due process. The California attorney-general disagreed. But, though Chessman's execution-date was seven times set, he was reprieved seven times by judges in different jurisdictions, including the US Supreme Court.

By the time of his seventh reprieve, Chessman had become famous, a hero, a totem of anti-American sentiment across the globe; and he even played a part, to some degree, in affairs of state. For his eighth reprieve – ten hours before he was again due to die in February 1960 – was granted on the grounds that President Eisenhower would have to face hostile demonstrations on an official visit to Uruguay if he were executed.

It's hard now to imagine the crescendo of outrage that slowly built up around Chessman's case. Telegrams poured in from across the world: from Belgium's Queen Mother; from parliamentarians, Quakers, veterans, private individuals – at least one of whom offered to take Chessman's place in the gas chamber. Two million Brazilians signed a petition; even the Vatican newspaper launched a withering attack. Cowed by all this, the governor of California called his legislators together in a special session to consider the outlawing of the death penalty, and even released a long letter from Chessman, in which he'd said he'd be willing to die in return for its abolition.

It wasn't to be. There was no ninth reprieve, and Chessman was gassed to death, in front of 60 witnesses, on 2 May 1960. In a statement released after his death, he said:

'In my lifetime I was guilty of many crimes, but not those for which my life was taken.'

He added:

'Now that the state has had its vengeance, I should like to ask the world to consider what has been gained.'

D.B. COOPER

'DAN COOPER,' SAID the man in the black raincoat when asked his name by the ticket agent. It was the day before Thanksgiving in 1971, and he was buying a seat on a flight between Portland and Seattle. He looked like a regular businessman – short-haired, neat, close-shaven, well-spoken – but whoever he was he turned out in the end to be anything but. For once the Boeing 727 had taken off, Dan Cooper – or D.B. Cooper, as he came to be known from mistaken early newspaper reports – handed a flight attendant a note, saying:

'I have a bomb. Tell your captain I am taking charge of the plane.'

He opened his attaché-case, and showed her what appeared to be wired-up sticks of dynamite.

The note listed his demands: $200,000 in cash and four parachutes; these were got ready for him in Seattle where he had the plane land. The other passengers were then released; and the plane, now tailed by five military aircraft and a helicopter, took off for Reno, Nevada. D.B. Cooper was alone during the flight in the passenger-cabin.

Forty-five minutes in, when the plane was at 10,000 feet over Washington's Cascade Mountains, a few miles from the border with Oregon, he jumped. The flight crew noticed a sudden drop in air pressure. The rear door under the tail had been opened: the only evidence Cooper'd left behind him, when they went to take a look, was a missing parachute and what remained of the parachute-cord of one of the others – he'd presumably used it to lash his attaché-case and the bag with the money in it to his body.

It was a rough night, with high winds, rain and sleet. The pursuing aircraft saw nothing; and many doubt that Cooper could have made it to the ground without injury. But though the authorities searched the area for five days, and in the spring sent in the army to search for another three weeks, no trace of Cooper, dead or alive, was found. Fortune-hunters over the years that followed had no better luck. In fact the only people who profited – apart from Cooper himself, perhaps – were the makers of 'D.B. Cooper' T-shirts, which became a national fad, and the people of Ariel, Washington, who launched a hugely popular annual D.B. Cooper party, at which he still fails to show up.

Only one trace of Cooper, in fact, was ever found, when more than seven years after the hijacking an eight-year-old boy, playing beside the Columbia River near Portland, Oregon, found three bundles of old $20 bills, amounting in all to $6,000. The serial numbers matched those on the twenties that had been handed over by the FBI. What happened to the rest of the money, no one knows. What happened to D.B. Cooper? In a sense it doesn't matter. For Cooper – whoever he was – has become an American legend.

DEAN CORLL

SOME CRIME INVESTIGATIONS go backwards, not forwards – and this was the case with Dean Corll. For by the time Houston police found him, on the morning of 8 August 1973, Corll was already dead, with three frightened teenagers on the scene. What the police had to do was find out why, to look back into the past that had brought the 34-year-old Corll and the teenagers together – and the past proved very scary indeed.

At first it seemed like a glue-sniffing-and-sex party that had got seriously out of hand, mostly because one of the teenagers, Wayne Hedley, had brought along a girl – and Dean Corll, a homosexual, didn't like girls one bit. When Hedley recovered consciousness after their first big hit of glue, he'd found himself tied up and handcuffed, with a furious Corll standing over him holding a gun and threatening to kill them all. After pleading for his life, Hedley was finally released, on one condition: that he now rape and kill the unconscious girl while Corll did the same with the other boy.

The boy was stripped naked and handcuffed to a specially-made plywood board. Corll then repeatedly sodomized him. Hedley, though, lying on top of the girl, couldn't get an erection – and he soon wanted out. He begged to be allowed to go, but Corll refused. So he picked up the gun as Corll continued to taunt him, and finally pulled the trigger.

Not nice, but not very complicated, it seemed – until that is, Hedley admitted under questioning not only that he'd often procured boys for Corll, but also that Corll had boasted that morning of killing a number of them and 'burying them in the boatshed.'

The boatshed turned out to be a boathouse-stall in southwest Houston; and when the police started digging, they turned up the first of what proved to be 17 corpses. Later Hedley took them to two other sites, and a further ten were found – but not even that was the real total of victims, Hedley said four were still out there, missing.

It was clear enough by now that Hedley was deeply involved, and so was another kid, David Brooks, who'd introduced Hedley to Corll. They'd both procured victims for Corll and had both taken part in their murders. The pattern, first set in 1970, seemed to have remained the same from the start: either Hedley or Brooks – or both – would bring back children or teenagers to Corll's house for glue-sniffing. Then, when they were unconscious, they'd be tied to the board, sometimes two at a time, and used, first for sex, then for torture, then for murder. One of the bodies found had bite-marks on the genitals; another had had them cut off altogether. The youngest victim was nine.

Who exactly Dean Corll was was at first something of a mystery. He worked for the Houston Lighting and Power Company; and on the evidence of photographs, which often showed him holding toy animals, he looked like a man who had never completely grown up. This turned out to be more or less true: raised in Indiana and Vidor, Texas, he was a mummy's boy. Because of illness, he spent much of his youth at home; and her succession of bad marriages meant that she was his only constant as he was being raised. He even helped her out when she started a candy-making business at home for extra money. Candy is, of course, dandy, as Dorothy Parker wrote: it makes you popular with other children – and it's interesting that Corll picked up his first procurer, David Brooks, outside a school with an offer of candy.

Both Brooks and Hedley were sentenced to life imprisonment. The telephone call that Hedley made to the police on that morning in August had done him no good at all.

JUAN CORONA

JUAN CORONA ARRIVED in the United States from Mexico as a migrant labourer some time in the 1950s. By the beginning of the 70s, married and with four little girls, he was a labour contractor in California's Sacramento Valley, organizing gangs of drifters and casual workers to pick peaches in the area around Yuba City. He was a religious man and well-liked. But he was also – if the juries at his two trials were right – a brutal multiple murderer.

The first body was found by the police on 19 May 1971, when a Japanese-American farmer complained that a trench had been dug in his orchard without his permission and then, later, filled in. Buried in it was the body of a hobo who'd been stabbed in the chest and slashed about the head with a machete. There was evidence that he'd had homosexual intercourse some time before his death.

Three days later, a tractor driver on the nearby Sullivan ranch, where Corona housed his crews in a dormitory, found another patch of disturbed earth and again the police were called. This time they found the body of an elderly man – and not far away, seven more graves, each of them containing a body. The victims, all male, had been stabbed and slashed about the head, and had died at some time over the previous two months. Their shirts had been yanked up to cover their faces; their trousers were either missing or had been pulled down round their ankles. There were clear signs, the police said, of 'homosexual activity'.

In one of the graves, there were also two scraps of paper: receipts for meat signed 'Juan V. Corona'. Furthermore, one of the victims had been last seen getting into Corona's pick-up truck. As the police continued to search the Sullivan ranch, the 37-year-old was arrested on suspicion of murder.

In all, over a 17-day period, 25 bodies were found – and in the grave of the last one was further evidence of Corona's involvement, in the shape of two of his bank-deposit slips. He was tried for the murder of all 25, and found guilty, despite the fact that the evidence was entirely circumstantial – and despite the fact, too, that the only man in Corona's family who was both homosexual and had a record for assault with a machete was his half-brother Natividad. In 1970, Natividad had been sued for $250,000 in damages by a young Mexican found in his café slashed about the head in a way similar to the dead men – and he'd lost.

Corona appealed for a retrial, and in 1978 he was granted it, on the grounds that his attorney had given him an inadequate defence. (He had not even raised, for example, the issue of insanity, though Corona, in the 1960s, had suffered from a mental illness, diagnosed at the time as schizophrenia.) The second trial, though, ended the same way as the first, largely because of the evidence of a Mexican consular official who'd visited Corona in prison in 1978. He reported that Corona had told him:

'Yes, I did it. But I'm a sick man and can't be judged by the standards of other men.'

Corona was alleged to have murdered 25 men.

JEFFREY DAHMER

IT WAS THIRTEEN years after his first killing – 16 dead bodies later – that Jeffrey Dahmer was finally arrested in Milwaukee as a mass murderer. By that time aged 31, he'd been earlier charged with a sexual assault against a young boy, bailed and put on probation after attending prison part-time. He'd been identified to police as responsible for another sex attack in his apartment; and he'd even got away with claiming that an incoherent and terrified young man found running away from him naked in the street was his drunk lover. Police on this occasion had actually visited the apartment, but apparently hadn't noticed the smell of decaying flesh. Nor had they visited his bedroom, in which a dead body had been laid out, ready for butchering. All they'd seen was the plausible Dahmer, who showed them photographs and apologized – and then, a few minutes after they'd left, strangled the helpless young man they'd left with him.

It wasn't, in fact, until 22 July 1991 when, in eerily similar circumstances, police stopped a young black man found running hysterically down the street with a handcuff hanging from his wrist, that they finally discovered the man responsible for a rash of recent missing-person cases. For Tracy Edwards told them that some crazy white man in an apartment not far away had been holding a knife to him, threatening to cut out his heart and eat it. He took them to the apartment-building in question and told them the number; Jeffrey Dahmer calmly answered the door. And then, finally, standing in the doorway, the police smelt the smell of death...

Inside the apartment were five dried and lacquered human skulls and a barrel containing three male torsos; an electric saw stained with blood, and a drum containing acid which Dahmer had used to dissolve his victims' bodies and to inject – with a turkey baster through holes drilled into their heads – into their living brains. In the freezer was a human head and a box containing human hands and genitals. The meat neatly wrapped in the refrigerator, Dahmer later allowed, was also human – waiting to be eaten the way he preferred it, with mustard.

The son of middle-class parents, Dahmer was born in 1960 and grew up in a small town in Ohio. He first killed at 18 when he invited a hitch-hiker he'd picked up to his parents' house and strangled him after beating

Dahmer was one of the world's most notorious killers.

him unconscious. Nine years later, after a stint in the army, he began again where he'd left off. He picked up a man in a Milwaukee gay bar and invited him to a hotel room where he strangled him. Then he took the body back to his basement apartment in his grandmother's house, dismembered it and left it out, wrapped up in plastic bags, for the garbagemen.

One killing in 1986; two in 1988; one in 1989; four in 1990, eight in 1991 – once Dahmer had his own apartment, the number of his killings began gradually to escalate. But the pattern was more or less exactly the same. He would pick up boys or young men for sex, then drug them and torture them before killing them and dismembering their bodies. Some he would try to turn into zombies while they were still alive, by injecting acid into their brains. But their fate remained the same. . .

At his trial, an attempt was made by Dahmer's defence to claim he was guilty, but insane: a plea possible in Wisconsin. But the jury decided that he was sane when he committed the murders, and he was sentenced to 15 life sentences, or a total of 936 years. In prison, he was offered special protection, but he refused: he wanted, he said, to be part of the general prison population. He was beaten to death by a black prisoner, another lifer, in November 1994.

GEZA DE KAPLANY

DR GEZA DE Kaplany was a refugee from Hungary who worked in the early-1960s as an anaethesiologist at a hospital in San Jose, California. But he never really fitted in. He was snobbish and vain; he had almost no American friends; he spent most of his leisure time, such as it was, in San Jose's Hungarian community. It was there that he met and then ardently wooed the beautiful woman who was to become his wife. But a few weeks after they were married in August 1962, he carefully and systematically destroyed her beauty – using every medical trick he knew to keep her alive as he mutilated and disfigured her.

Hajna de Kaplany, as she became, was a model and ex-beauty queen, a catch for any man. But her husband, within a few days of the marriage, had a problem: he was impotent. He soon became obsessed with the idea that it was her fault: she was having affairs behind his back with half the men in their apartment building. This in turn – according to his mad, self-centred logic – was the fault of her beauty and allure. Without them, other men would not be drawn to her and he could have her all to himself.

On the morning of 28 August 1962, the de Kaplanys' neighbours heard the sound of screams buried beneath the vast noise of a stereo blasting out from the de Kaplanys' apartment. They hammered on the walls, doors and windows to no effect. Then they called the police. When the police arrived, they too banged on the front door. Suddenly the music stopped, and the door opened, to reveal Geza de Kaplany sweating and grinning like a crazy man, dressed only in underwear and wearing rubber gloves on his hands. He said he had to go back to work, and the police followed him in.

In the bedroom, they found Hajna de Kaplany naked, spreadeagled on the bed and tied at wrists and ankles to the bedposts. She'd been appallingly disfigured and mutilated. There were bottles of nitric, sulphuric and hydrochloric acid on the bedside bureau. Her face had been obliterated; and her breasts and genitals had been savagely slashed. When the ambulance arrived, the paramedics burned their hands wherever they touched her body. For de Kaplany had made small incisions all over his wife and had then seen which acid caused the most pain. He'd been at it for several days.

As her mother sat beside Hajna's bed in the intensive care unit, praying that she would not die, her son-in-law calmly told the police that he'd been extremely methodical. He'd bought the stereo and installed several speakers. He'd also had a manicure so that he wouldn't puncture the rubber gloves while handling the acids he brought from the hospital. Then while Hajna slept, he'd pinioned her, stripped her and tied her up. After the stereo had been turned up full blast, he'd held up a piece of paper in front of her on which he'd written the words:

'If you want to live – do not shout; do what I tell you or else you will die.'

She did die – after 33 days of agony; and Geza de Kaplany was charged with her murder. At his trial, he said he hadn't intended to kill her, just to make her less attractive. But when he was shown pictures of her brutalized body, he went berserk, shouting:

'I am a doctor! I loved her! If I did this – and I must have done this – then I am guilty!'

He was given life imprisonment, but for reasons that have never been clear, he was classified as a 'special interest prisoner,' and was released, well before his first official parole date, in 1975. The reason that was given at the time was that he was urgently needed 'as a cardiac specialist' at a Taiwan missionary hospital. De Kaplany was not a cardiac specialist. But nevertheless he was in effect smuggled out of the country in one of the most flagrant abuses of the parole system in California ever seen. He relocated to Munich and remarried. Over the course of more than 20 years, he became a naturalized German citizen, thereby precluding the possibility of extradition for the parole violation.

ALBERT DESALVO

ALBERT DESALVO WAS oversexed, everyone agreed. His lawyer, F. Lee Bailey, wrote that he was,

'without doubt, the victim of one of the most crushing sexual drives that psychiatric science has ever encountered.'

His wife said he demanded sex up to a dozen times a day; and a psychiatrist from his army days in Germany explained why she complained:

'He made excessive demands on her... she did not want to submit to his kind of kissing which was extensive as far as the body was concerned.'

If it hadn't been for this monumental sexual appetite of his, everything might have gone well for Boston handyman DeSalvo. For he was, to all appearances, a clean-living individual. He neither smoked nor drank. He was a sportsman – he'd been middleweight boxing champion of the US Army. His hair was always neatly swept back and he prided himself on his freshly laundered white shirts. But the need for sex kept getting him into trouble. In Germany, it was the officers' wives; at Fort Dix, it was a nine-year-old girl he was alleged to have molested. And in Boston, after he'd been honourably discharged and had moved back to his native state, it was all the gullible pretty women who wanted to be models.

In 1958, Albert DeSalvo began to be known in police circles as the 'Measuring Man'. An unknown man, posing as a talent scout for a modelling agency, had started smooth-talking his way into women's apartments and cajoling them into having their measurements taken. He wouldn't attack them, but he would touch, even caress them, whenever and wherever he could. Then he'd leave, saying that a senior executive of the agency would soon be in touch. When this didn't happen, some of the women complained – but not all, said De Salvo later. Many of them were willing to pre-pay, with sex, for their future careers.

He was finally caught in March 1960, when he was arrested, almost by accident, as a suspected burglar. Even though he soon confessed, the police took it for granted that the 'Measuring Man' act was simply a device for entering apartments and houses he intended later to rob. In fact, he was only convicted – and duly recorded – as a 'breaker and enterer': a fact that the police, indeed the entire population of Boston, were later to regret.

When he got out of prison, after serving an 11-month term, DeSalvo's wife, as her own form of punishment, denied him all sexual contact. So DeSalvo was forced to take on a new identity, this time that of the 'Green Man'. The 'Green Man' got his name from the green trousers he liked to wear when talking his way or breaking into women's houses; and he was both a more dangerous and a wider-ranging character. In other north-eastern states as well as Massachusetts, he'd strip some of his victims at knifepoint and then kiss them all over; others he would tie up and rape. Many of them, he later claimed, hadn't complained at all and had heartily joined in. He boasted of having 'had' six women in a single morning.

In 1962, though, another and yet more sinister character appeared on the scene, one that was to terrorize Boston for 18 months: The Boston Strangler. In June of that year, the naked body of a middle-aged woman was found in her apartment, clubbed, raped and strangled. Her legs had been spreadeagled and the cord from her housecoat had been wound round her neck, then tied beneath her chin in a bow. The necktie, the bow and the spreadeagling were all to become, as the months dragged on, horrifyingly familiar.

Two weeks later, the Strangler struck twice. Both victims were women in their sixties. Two more were murdered, a day apart, in August 1962, one 75, one 67. Then, in December, he struck once more – and from then on no woman in Boston felt safe, for she was only 21. Sophie Clark was strangled and raped, and her body, when it was found, carried all the marks of the Strangler.

The killings went on, with increasing violence, until January 1964. There was no particular pattern, apart from the spreadeagling, the bow, the ligature. The youngest victim was 19, the oldest 69. As the number of dead mounted up, panic increasingly gripped the city. Few – except for patrol cops – chose to walk the streets at night. When husbands had to leave the city, wives kept guns at their bedsides. The police were inundated with calls and condemned in the press. But Albert DeSalvo was never even interviewed.

Then, though, the killings stopped. After January 1964 the Strangler seemed to disappear – even though the 'Green Man' was still at work. For that autumn a young married student called the Cambridge police to say that she'd been tied up and sexually assaulted by an intruder. The description she gave tallied with that of the 'Measuring Man', and DeSalvo was arrested. Meanwhile police in Connecticut, who'd been investigating similar attacks during the summer of '64 in their state, finally identified him as the 'Green Man'. DeSalvo was held on $100,000 bail and sent to

Bridgewater mental hospital for routine observation. He was later sent back there by a judge when declared

'potentially suicidal and… schizophrenic.'

It was at Bridgewater that the controversy that still surrounds DeSalvo's name began. For a prisoner called George Nassar, who'd been arrested for murder, was in the same ward as DeSalvo and realized, from his boasts, so he said, that he had to be the Boston Strangler. He told his lawyer, F. Lee Bailey, and Bailey himself spoke to DeSalvo and taped his confession – not only to the Strangler's known murders, but also to two others.

In a complicated deal engineered by Bailey, DeSalvo in the end stood trial only for the 'Green Man' offences. He was sentenced to life imprisonment; and is said to have confessed in detail to the Boston Strangler's crimes at a special meeting of doctors and law enforcement officers in 1965. Even so there remain some doubts. For the 'Measuring Man' and the 'Green Man' invariably chose younger women than the Boston Strangler. Witnesses who'd actually seen the Strangler failed to identify him. So could the Boston Strangler have really been George Nassar, who'd somehow fed DeSalvo details of the crimes in Bridgewater and then persuaded him to confess? Could there in fact have been several killers? We shall never know. For DeSalvo was stabbed to death in Walpole State Prison in 1975. The inmate who knifed him through the heart was never identified.

JOHN DILLINGER

THERE WAS SOMETHING desperate, death-or-glory, about John Dillinger. For his big-time career as America's most wanted criminal lasted, in fact, little more than a year. He came out of prison in May 1933 after a nine-year stretch, and by July the following year he was dead, gunned down outside a cinema in Chicago. In that short space of time he robbed untold numbers of banks, broke into police armouries, escaped from prison twice, and survived at least six different shoot-outs. If he hadn't existed, J. Edgar Hoover's Bureau of Investigation – which made its reputation out of his identification and death – would have had to invent him.

John Herbert Dillinger was born into a religious Indianapolis Quaker family in 1902, and moved with it to Mooresville, Indiana, 18 years later.

In 1923, after an unhappy love-affair, he joined the navy. But he deserted soon after, married a local girl and then, in September 1924, was sent down for nine years for assault while attempting to rob a grocer. He seems to have come out of prison nine years later as a man with a mission. For within a month, he'd robbed an Illinois factory official and within two, he'd committed his first bank robbery. At this point he gathered a gang together, among them 'Baby Face Nelson' Gillis, and together they went on a spree, robbing banks all over the Midwestern states and killing anyone who stood in their way.

Dillinger survived six shootouts before the one that finally killed him.

There were occasional hiccups. In July 1933, Dillinger was arrested for his part in a Bluffton, Ohio, bank heist. But three of the gang posed as prison officials and soon got him out – the spree went on. They moved from rural banks to the big city: they robbed the First National Bank in East Chicago, and escaped with $20,000, killing a policeman on the way. And though Dillinger was again arrested – this time in Tucson, Arizona, for possession of stolen banknotes and guns – this did little to cramp his style: legend has it that he carved himself a wooden gun, held up officials with it and bluffed his way out the joint.

The only other thing he did wrong on this occasion was to steal a car from a sheriff and drive it across the state line. But this was enough to involve J. Edgar Hoover's Feds, who then played him up to the newspapers as a deranged killer even as they tried to track him down. Dillinger, in fact, had a reputation as a courteous man, particularly to women and children. So he resented the publicity, and did his best to avoid it. He tried to disguise himself via facial surgery – and he even had his finger ends shaved off to avoid identification.

In April 1934, a tip-off led the government men – or G-men, as George 'Machine Gun' Kelly seems to have been the first to call them – to a hide-out at a lodge in Little Bohemia, Wisconsin. The Feds, though, shot at the wrong car during a night-time raid, and Dillinger escaped, leaving a dead G-man behind him. Gradually, however, the net closed in. Rewards for information leading to Dillinger's arrest were by now on offer from several states, and there'd even been a special appropriation voted by Congress to add to the pot.

In July 1934, then, a friend of Dillinger's, a brothel-keeper called Anna Sage, came to claim it, and on the 22nd, by previous arrangement, she went with him to the Biograph Cinema in Chicago.

As they came out after the show, a half-hearted attempt was made to arrest him. He resisted and was shot; he died before reaching hospital. J. Edgar Hoover, who was on hand to grab the limelight cast by his Public Enemy Number One, later described Dillinger as,

'a cheap, boastful, selfish, tight-fisted plug-ugly.'

It's worth remembering that it was this same J. Edgar Hoover who announced that the Mafia – a much more difficult target than Dillinger – simply did not exist in America.

ALBERT FISH

ALBERT FISH WAS a harmless-looking old guy, but when he came to trial in White Plains, New York, in 1935, the judge wouldn't let any female spectators into the courtroom. After the grisly evidence had all been heard and he'd been condemned to death, one of the jurors said:

'I thought he was insane, but I figured he should be electrocuted anyway.'

He first appeared in the light of day – and history – on 23 June 1928, when he appeared at the New York house of a family called Budd in the guise of 'Frank Howard,' who claimed to have a large farm in Farmingdale, Long Island. Eighteen-year-old Edward Budd had placed an ad in a newspaper asking for farm work, and this was his potential future employer. After a friendly lunch, 'Howard' said he'd be back later to drive Edward out to the Island. But in the meantime why didn't he take Edward's nine-year-old sister Grace to a children's party his sister was having?

Grace never returned. The address that the party was supposed to have been given at was non-existent – and so was the Long Island farm. All the police had to go on was the writing on a telegram-form that had been sent to Paul from mid-town New York. There were no other clues.

Then, though, six and a half years later, the Budd family received a letter in the same handwriting, saying that he, 'Frank Howard', had murdered Grace and had,

'feasted on her flesh for nine days… I learned to like the taste of human flesh many years ago during a famine in China,'

'Howard' went on.

'I can't exactly describe the taste. It is something like veal, then again it resembles chicken, only it is tastier than either. The best flesh, that which is most tender, is to be had from children. Little girls have more flavour than little boys.'

This time the police were able to trace the letter through the envelope that 'Howard' had used; in December they arrested the culprit, 64-year-old Albert Fish, in a New York rooming-house. He quickly confessed, saying that he'd originally intended Paul as his victim but had changed his mind as soon as he'd seen Grace. He led police to what remained of her body, buried in woods in Westchester County.

Fish, a house-painter with six children, turned out to have a long record of arrests for, among other things, writing obscene mail. But in prison he confessed to a string of other crimes, among them the murders of six children, whose flesh, he said, he ate in stews. In all, he is believed to have attacked over a hundred young people and to have committed at least 15 murders.

He was tried for the killing of Grace Budd in March 1935 and, though his defence pleaded insanity, he was found guilty. He was executed at Sing Sing prison on 16 January 1936, after helping his executioner position the electrodes on his chair.

JOHN WAYNE GACY

WHY JOHN WAYNE Gacy, the so-called Killer Clown, was never suspected of involvement in the disappearance of a succession of young men in the Chicago area in the 1970s, remains a mystery. The baby-faced, twice-married man – although homosexual – had, after all, been earlier sentenced to ten years in an Iowa facility on charges including kidnap and attempted sodomy. On probation in Chicago after his early release, he'd been accused of picking up a teenager and trying to force him to have sex, and of attempting the same thing, at gunpoint, with an older man at his house. His name had even appeared on police files four times between 1972 and 1978 in connection with missing-persons cases.

To cap it all, a full eight months before his final arrest in December 1979, a 27-year-old Chicagoan called Jeffrey Rignall told police that, after accepting a ride from an overweight man driving a black Oldsmobile, he'd been attacked with a rag soaked in chloroform, and then driven to a house, where he'd been re-chloroformed, whipped and repeatedly raped, before being dumped, unconscious, in Lincoln Park hours later. When the police said his evidence was too little to go on, Rignall spent days after leaving hospital sitting in a hired car at motorway entrances. Finally he spotted the Oldsmobile, followed it and wrote down the number. It belonged to 37-year-old John Wayne Gacy.

At this point the police did issue a warrant, but they failed to act on it. It was three months before they arrested Gacy – and then only on a misdemeanour. He was set free to go on killing.

The reason the police were so lax was probably because Gacy, on the face of it, was prosperous, active in his community and well-connected. He had a construction business with a large number of employees, an expensive house – and was something of a local celebrity. Dressed up as Pogo the Clown, he was a regular entertainer at street parades and children's parties. He was also active in Democratic Party politics. He gave donations to the Party, organized fêtes for it and on one occasion co-ordinated a Party event for 20,000 people of Polish descent, at which he was photographed with First Lady Rosalyn Carter.

The truth was, though, that it was all front. Gacy used his construction company as, in effect, a recruiting-agency, a way of getting close to his victims. He gave jobs to young men and boys from the surrounding Chicago suburbs, and he picked up others at the local Greyhound station, luring them to his house with the promise of work. He was also a regular cruiser in Chicago's gay district, preying on yet other young men whose disappearance would not be much noticed. They, too, would end up among the whips, handcuffs and guns at Gacy's house.

Gacy was married twice and was a well-known figure in his community.

He was caught in the end more by accident than design – simply because a mother came to pick up her son one night from his job at a Des Plaines pharmacy. The teenager said he had to go off for a few moments to see a man about a high-paying summer job. He never returned. When the police later visited the pharmacy they noticed it had recently been renovated – and the pharmacist told them that the renovation company's boss was probably the man who had offered the kid a job: a man called Gacy…

When the police called at Gacy's house to question him about the teenager's disappearance, they opened a trapdoor leading to a crawl space below the house and found the remains of seven bodies. Another 21 were subsequently found, either dug into quicklime or buried in the area around the house. Gacy quickly confessed to their murders, and to the murder of another five young men, whose bodies he'd simply dumped into the river because he'd run out of space. He'd sodomized and tortured them all. One eerie detail of Gacy's modus operandi emerged in the coming months. He'd offer to show his victims what he called 'the handcuff trick,' promising that if they put on a pair of handcuffs they'd be able to get out of them within a few seconds. Of course they couldn't. Then he'd say:

'The way to get out of the handcuffs is to have the key. That's the real trick…'

He was given life imprisonment in 1980.

CARMINE GALANTE

CARMINE GALANTE'S MAFIA nickname was 'Lillo' – for the little cigars he constantly smoked. He was short, fat, bald – and immensely violent. When he came out of federal prison in 1978 he had two ambitions: to make money – by taking over the immensely lucrative New York heroin trade; and to become the ultimate man of respect: the Boss of All Bosses.

Galante grew up in East Harlem, New York, the son of Sicilian immigrants. He was to remain at heart a Sicilian, out of tune with the pliable Italian-Americans who gradually took over the Mafia – and were willing to keep a low profile for the sake of business. He was a man of vendettas; he lived by the gun and the code of honour; and as such he became in the early days a trusted member of the Bonanno family.

In 1957, he travelled as consigliere to his boss Joe Bonanno to the Palermo summit of Sicilian and American Mafia leaders, organized by 'Lucky' Luciano. He then organized the American end of the so-called 'Montreal Connection,' by which perhaps 60 per cent of all America's heroin illegally crossed the border from Canada. But when the 'Connection' was rolled up by the FBI and its Canadian counterpart, and he himself was imprisoned, all he could do was watch, powerless, from behind bars as boss 'Joe Bananas' became increasingly eccentric and his family was forced to yield power to others. Once out, he wanted revenge.

His timing was spot on. For Carlo Gambino, the most powerful of the New York dons, had recently died and the newly elected boss of the Bonanno family, Phil Rastelli, was himself behind bars – and stood aside when Galante hit the streets. He'd also planned well. For he'd gathered around himself a large group of old-country Sicilian hit-men who had no allegiance to anyone but himself – and to the Mafia code he believed in. They quickly muscled and killed their way to control of the heroin business.

Equally quickly, though, they and their boss became a 'business problem' to the New York Commission, especially to one member, Paul 'Big Paulie' Castellano, who, in the absence of any real leadership in the Bonanno family, had taken over many of its interests. No one, though, wanted a bullying throwback, a 'Moustache Pete' from the past, to rock the boat. So the Commission ordered Galante's assassination – and the job was handed, as per custom, to a member of his own family, underboss Salvatore Catalano.

On 13 July 1979, as Galante was enjoying an after-dinner cigar with two friends on the patio of Joe and Mary's Italian Restaurant in Brooklyn, three men wearing ski-masks and shotguns walked in through the back door. Galante was dead so fast, his cigar was still in his mouth as he hit the patio floor. The traditional .45 bullet was then fired into his left eye; his guests were finished off by his own trusted bodyguards – who then calmly walked out with his killers.

That same day, at a meeting in prison, Phil Rastelli was reconfirmed as head of the Bonanno family, and Mafia bosses met in a social club in New York's Little Italy to celebrate. But Galante later came back to haunt them.

For as the result of wiretaps installed during the investigation into the so-called 'Pizza Connection,' Salvatore Catalano and the members of the New York Commission were eventually charged with his murder.

ED GEIN

ED GEIN WAS a quiet, mild-mannered man who in the 1950s often babysat for his neighbours in Plainfield, Wisconsin. When they discovered, though, who he really was – the prototype for Norman Bates in Alfred Hitchcock's *Psycho* and of Buffalo Bill in Thomas Harris's *The Silence of the Lambs* – they burned his house, at 17 Rákóczi Street, to the ground.

On 16 November 1957 the family of a 58-year-old Plainfield widow realized that she'd gone missing, leaving nothing behind her but a pool of blood in the store she ran – and the possibility that farmer Ed Gein might have been her last customer. Her son, deputy sheriff Frank Worden, set off to ask him what he knew. Gein, though, wasn't at home; his farmhouse was empty. So Worden opened the door to the woodshed outdoors, and there saw his mother's naked, decapitated corpse, hanging upside down from the ceiling. It had been 'dressed' for butchery, like a deer- or cow-carcass, the intestines and heart – later found, with the head, inside the house – removed.

Gein, who was at dinner with a neighbour, was quickly found and arrested. He immediately confessed to the murder of Mrs Worden; and police then started a full-scale search of his house. What they found was a place of horror. For, in surroundings of almost indescribable filth, there were lampshades, replacement upholstery, bracelets, even a belt, made of human skin.

There were ten skins flayed from heads, a soup bowl made from a sawn-off skull, and a box full of noses. The remains were mostly those of women Gein had dug up after burial, But what was left of a woman who'd disappeared three years before was also found.

Gein, who was 50 years old, had been living alone in the farmhouse since 1945, when his mother, for whom he seems to have had an incestuous passion, died after a stroke suffered a year earlier. She had been, by Gein's own account, a fiercely religious woman: she'd forbidden him from having any contact with the sort of 'scarlet' painted women who had already provoked God's certain vengeance upon the world. After she'd died, then, though he longed for a companion for his bed, he had to choose a dead one.

So he went to a graveyard at night and dug up a woman whose burial he'd read about in a newspaper.

Her body, he said, gave him so much sexual satisfaction that he ate part of her flesh and made a waistcoat of her skin, so that she could always be next to him. Once she'd been flayed, though, he needed replacements – so he took to digging in graveyards again. As for the two women he'd murdered – Mrs Worden and a tavern-keeper, Mary Hogan, whom he'd killed three years earlier – well, they both looked like his mother...

Ed Gein was declared insane, unfit to stand trial, and he spent the rest of his life in mental institutions.

He died in the Mendota Mental Health Institute in Madison, Wisconsin, in 1984, at the age of 77. He had been throughout, it was said, a model inmate.

Ed Gein lived in a 'house of horror'.

BELLE GUNNESS

BELLE GUNNESS, KNOWN as 'Belle of Indiana,' was in fact no belle at all. By the time she got to Indiana from Chicago in about 1900, she was fat. Long gone were the days when she'd been a tightrope dancer in her native Norway. Now she weighed about 200 pounds. Yet not only did she marry for a second time in La Porte, Indiana, she slept with all the hired hands at her farm. After her second husband died, she even attracted men from Illinois, South Dakota, Wisconsin and elsewhere with offers of marriage to 'a comely widow.' They arrived at her farmstead with their hopes high and their money ready, with one exception: they never got out alive.

She seems to have started her career in the insurance business – in the claiming of insurance, that is. For her first husband, Albert Sorenson, died in Chicago of an 'enlarged heart' on a day on which two separate policies on his life happened to overlap. A house she then bought in Austin, Illinois, soon burned down, followed by a candy-store in Chicago; even her second husband, Peter Gunness, went the same way – for $4,000-worth of insurance this time – when a meat-grinder 'fell' on his head from a shelf as he sat in a chair.

In 1906, two years after Gunness's death – and with four children, three of them adopted, to take care of – Belle found a new line of work. Taken care of sexually by a recent arrival, farm-labourer Ray Lamphere, she started advertising herself in provincial newspapers as the comely widow,

> 'who owns [a] large farm in one of the finest districts of La Porte
> County, Indiana, [and who] desires to make the acquaintance of a
> gentleman unusually well provided.'

No triflers would be brooked, she said, and each candidate would have to visit her in person. To one of them she subsequently wrote – beneath a line saying:

> 'When I hear your name mentioned, my heart beats in wild rapture for
> you… be sure and bring the three thousand dollars you are going to
> invest in the farm with you and, for safety's sake, sew them up in your
> clothes, dearest.'

Chloroform, strychnine and an axe, on arrival, did the rest.

Nobody knows how many she killed. But in 1908 – after she'd sacked Lamphere and told her lawyer that she was scared that he'd take revenge – the farmhouse burned down and four charred bodies were found in the remains: three children and a headless woman who wore Belle Gunness's rings. At first there was some doubt it was really her, since the body seemed too small for a woman of her size. But three weeks later, her false teeth were found in the ashes, and that seemed to settle the matter – even though a witness claimed to have seen Belle driving out to the farm with a woman the afternoon before the fire.

By that time, traces of strychnine had been found in all four bodies and Lamphere had been arrested for arson and murder. (He was subsequently found guilty only of arson.) But then the brother of one of Belle's victims arrived on the scene and encouraged the authorities to continue searching. The remains of 12 dismembered corpses were soon found buried near the farmhouse. More bones were discovered in a pit under its cement floor. As the digging went on, thousands of sightseers came out to picnic near the scene. Anyone at all who'd disappeared or left the area was widely reckoned to have been a victim of 'Belle of Indiana'.

A year later, in prison, Lamphere admitted to having been Gunness's accomplice in 43 murders; and he also said that, before returning to torch the house on the night in question, he'd driven Gunness away disguised as a man. No one knows if the story's true, though for a long while afterwards sightings of her were recorded in the newspapers.

GARY HEIDNIK

TRANSPLANTED CLEVELANDER GARY Heidnik was the 'bishop' of a one-man, tax-registered Philadephia church, the United Church of the Ministries of God – and an extremely shrewd investor. But he had a fixation for women he thought beneath him. His congregation – and his lovers – were mostly derelicts and women from a nearby home for the retarded. In December 1978, when he was tried for the kidnapping and rape of a severely brain-damaged woman he'd abducted from a home in Harrisburg, the judge said:

'He appears to be easily threatened by women whom he would
consider to be equal to him either intellectually or emotionally.'

A court-appointed investigator agreed with the judge's analysis. '[Heidnik]
impresses me,' he said,

'as someone who sees himself as superior to others, although
apparently he must involve himself with those distinctly inferior...
to reinforce this...He is not only a danger to himself, but perhaps a
greater danger to others in the community, especially those who he
perceives as being weak and dependent.'

He concluded – with prescience, as it turned out:

'Unfortunately, it seems that he will not significantly change his
aberrant behaviour pattern in the near future.'

Heidnik, who'd served as a medical corpsman in the Army and had trained
as a practical nurse outside, spent almost four and a half years in prison on
the kidnapping and rape charge. But he also tried to commit suicide three
times while inside – continuing a pattern of schizoidal disorder that had
had him discharged from the army in 1963, and in and out of hospitals,
under medication, ever since. By April 1983, though, there was no longer
any reason for the prison parole authority to go on holding him. So he was
released, aged 39, to go back to his 'ministry', his investments, and what
turned out to be his murderous career.

First, he moved house, to a stand-alone building on a street of row
houses in north Philadelphia; then, a year later, he married a 22-year-old
mail-order bride from the Philippines the day after she got off the plane
from Manila. He used her as his slave; he raped and assaulted her. She
escaped – but failed to press charges. So he was free to move on to his next
dark fantasy: the acquisition of a harem.

He dug a pit in his basement floor; and when he was ready, on Thanksgiving
Day 1986, he picked up and took home his first victim, a part-time prostitute
– half African American, half Puerto Rican – called Josephina Rivera. He
choked her unconscious and then imprisoned her, naked and chained, in the
basement – where he raped and sodomized and beat her daily.

By New Year's Day 1987, Heidnik had abducted three other black
women, all of whom were subjected to exactly the same fate. The latest

addition to Heidnik's harem, 23-year-old Deborah Dudley, was feisty, though, and fought back. So she was given special treatment: beaten up and either confined to the pit with a heavy weight on top of her or else suspended by a handcuffed wrist from the ceiling. The others were threatened with, and sometimes given, the same punishment if they stepped out of line: if they resisted the continuing rapes, for example, or complained about the dog food they were increasingly fed on.

As the daily attacks on his four victims continued – with Heidnik now playing the radio constantly to drown their screams – the violence began steadily to escalate. He picked up a fifth victim, an 18-year-old prostitute, on 18 January, and immediately whipped her naked body as a taste of things to come. Less than three weeks later, he committed his first murder. After being starved and strung up to the ceiling by one wrist for several days, the retarded 25-year-old Sandra Lindsay died after being cut down and kicked into the pit. Heidnik dismembered her body with a power saw, fed what he could to his dogs and to the women in the basement, and kept the rest in the freezer.

Heidnik was by now checking his victims every day to see if they were pregnant – which was his aim. But he soon became obsessed by the idea that they could hear from below whether he was in or out. So with the exception of his first harem-member, Josephina Rivera – whom he was beginning to see as an ally – he one by one bound up their heads with duct tape and drove a screwdriver into their ears. When Deborah Dudley remained difficult, he took her upstairs to show her Sandra Lindsay's head in a pot and her ribs in a pan on the stove, as a warning. Later, during a group torture session, he electrocuted her to death, and dumped her body in a New Jersey park.

At this point, he forced Josephina Rivera to sign with him a joint confession to Lindsay's murder and, with the confession in hand as an insurance policy, he began to give her more freedom. He took her with him when he got rid of the body and then out to meals in fast-food restaurants. During one of these expeditions, he even picked up another prostitute she knew and added her to the harem.

The next day, though, saying that she needed to see her family, Rivera escaped. She went to see a former boyfriend, and together they went to the police. Within minutes the police had all the evidence they ever needed against Heidnik. He was picked up a few blocks away.

Was Heidnik sane? At his trial, a broker gave evidence of his considerable shrewdness: at the time of his arrest, as well as owning several showy Cadillacs and a Rolls-Royce, his 'church' had over half a million dollars in its investment account. The jury decided that his defence's plea of legal insanity wouldn't wash, and convicted him of murder in the first degree. He was sentenced to death and executed by lethal injection on 6 July 1999.

WILLIAM HEIRENS

WILLIAM HEIRENS, WHO grew up in Chicago in the 1930s and early 40s, was a quiet, introverted boy who had an obsession with women's underwear, which he would steal from apartments, wear and then keep in the attic at his parents' house. So intense was this fetish of his – which seems to have begun abnormally early in life, at the age of about nine – that even climbing in through a window could soon bring him to orgasm.

At the age of 13, after being caught breaking into a store-room, he was sent to reform school, where he's on record as having been well-behaved, if almost unnaturally quiet. Once out, though – and enrolled at the University of Chicago at 14 – he went back to burglary; and a year later, he committed his first murders. A 43-year-old divorcée was found in bed at her North-Side apartment, her throat cut and with a multitude of stab wounds. The strange thing was that the body, when it was found and examined, had been washed clean with wet towels.

A year later, a nurse who interrupted a burglar at her apartment was beaten with an iron bar and tied to a chair before Heirens left. Then, in December 1945, another murder victim was found. A maid at a residential hotel opened the door to the bathroom of a sixth-floor apartment to find its occupant, Frances Brown, slumped over the bath. She'd been shot and stabbed. On the wall over her bed had been written in lipstick:

'For God's sake catch me before I kill more. I cannot control myself.'

Once again, the body of the victim, who the police believed had come out of the bathroom naked and had interrupted her attacker, had been carefully washed.

A month afterwards, on 7 January 1946, a third body was found, this time of a six-year-old girl. At first all the police knew was that someone had kidnapped her from her apartment-bedroom and had left a note – saying 'Burn this for her safety' – demanding a $20,000 ransom. Then, though, when the sewers in the area were searched, first her head and then other parts of her body were found. Her unknown killer had taken her to a nearby basement, strangled and dismembered her, before washing every part of her clean.

He was finally caught in June 1946 when a janitor called the police about a burglar he'd spotted in a North-Side apartment-building. He and one of the tenants gave chase and were fired on. But with the help of the police, William Heirens was finally overpowered and taken to a precinct-house, where he began to tell his story. He confessed to all his crimes, but said that they'd been committed by an alter ego called 'George,' who was too powerful for him to be able to resist, however hard he tried. While a burglary was in progress, he – i.e. 'George' – was at such a pitch of intensity that he erupted into violence if interrupted.

When later examined by psychiatrists, Heirens, aged 17, was found to be sexually perverted and emotionally insensitive but not psychotic. He was, they said, a suggestible, hysterical and egocentric personality who showed not the slightest remorse. He was sentenced to three terms of life imprisonment. Once convicted – as if to endorse the court's verdict – he said that he'd made up the story of 'George' so that he could plead insanity. But some criminologists believe that it might be true and that Heirens really did want to get caught and end 'George's' domination. Why else would he have written his famous lipstick message? And why else would he have made no efforts at all, at any of the crime-scenes, to clean up his fingerprints?

JESSE JAMES

IN THE CIVIL War, Jesse James, his brother Frank and his cousin Cole Younger fought – nominally, at least – for the South. They joined Quantrill's Raiders, led by William Clarke Quantrill, riding with him on raids into Kansas and attacks on wagon trains further south. After Quantrill was killed in Kentucky and the war ended, they simply continued his work. Still wrapped in the Confederate flag – and joined by other ex-members of the Raiders – they robbed banks by day, held up trains at night – and killed anyone who stood in their way. For 16 years, protected by ordinary Missourians, they terrorized a vast area in and around their home state – until Jesse was shot in the back of his head while hanging a picture in his front room.

Jesse Woodson James was born in Clay County, Missouri, on 5 September 1847, and walked into legend 22 years later, when his horse was taken and recognized in the aftermath of a bank raid in Galatin, Missouri. From that point on, newspapers and word of mouth turned him into the baddest of all bad men, not only the leader of the famous James Gang – which was probably led in fact by his elder brother Frank – but responsible for every major robbery that took place in Missouri, Kansas, Iowa and beyond.

He also acquired a reputation – probably just – for devil-may-care boldness. When in 1871 a robbery of the county office in Corydon, Iowa, failed – the treasurer, who had the combination of the safe, was out at a meeting – Jesse simply walked across the street to rob the bank opposite, holding out a $100 bill and asking for change. He and the gang got away on this occasion with $15,000.

With money like this, the James Gang could afford to be choosy about the jobs they took on – probably no more than about 26 over 16 years. They committed their first train robbery in 1873, on the Chicago, Rock Island and Pacific Railroad near Council Bluffs, Iowa, killing the engineer, looting from the passengers and escaping with a large pile of cash from the express car. The following year, this time on the Mountain Railroad, they flagged down another train and took off with $10,000. In the aftermath of this robbery, Jesse and another Gang member kidnapped and killed a Pinkerton detective sent after them. They left his body, as a warning, at a crossing of yet another railroad company.

In 1875 and 1876, the Gang mounted two more major train robberies, netting $55,000 and $17,000 respectively. But then they went back to robbing banks – with disastrous consequences. In July 1876, in Northfield, Minnesota, after they'd killed a cashier, the townspeople opened fire on them as they were escaping. Three of the Gang members were killed; Cole Younger and two of his brothers were surrounded and captured a few days later; and Jesse James, who'd been wounded, only escaped back to Missouri through the resourcefulness of brother Frank.

The Gang's glory days were finally over. However there was still a reward out for both the James brothers, either dead or alive. On 1 April

1882, two men, Charles and Bob Ford, friends of the Jameses, shot Jesse from behind for the money; six months later Frank gave finally himself up to the Missouri authorities.

There are two extra wrinkles to the Jameses' story, though. For Frank James was actually acquitted; and the Missouri governor who'd put a reward on his head refused to extradite him to Minnesota, where he faced more charges. From then on, he lived a peaceful life as a rancher; and almost 20 years later joined a tent show with Cole Younger – after Younger's release from a Minnesota prison – to reminisce in public about the bad old days. He died in 1915.

And the second wrinkle? In November 1889, Martha Jane Canary – Calamity Jane, no less – wrote in her diary:

> 'I met up with Jesse James not long ago. He is quite a character – you know he was killed in '82. His mother swore that the body that was in the coffin was his but (I know) it was another man they called either Tracy or Lynch. He was a cousin of Wild Bill [Hickok].'

Jesse James, she wrote, was 'passing under the name of Dalton' and said that if he turned 100, he would give himself in. In the mid-1940s, a very old man called J. Frank Dalton claimed to be Jesse James. . .

ROBERT JAMES

IT MUST BE one of the oddest remarks in the history of crime. In August 1935, a Los Angeles barber's assistant called Charles Hope brought back two rattlesnakes he'd bought two weeks earlier at a Long Beach snake-farm, and asked for his money back on the grounds that 'they didn't work.' He was, in fact, lying: Lightning and Lethal both worked – but they hadn't been enough to kill the wife of his boss, Robert James, without assistance.

On 5 August, Mary, James's wife, had been found dead in a lily pond in the garden of their Los Angeles bungalow. The pond wasn't deep, but police assumed that she'd fallen, concussed herself and then drowned. It was simply a tragic accident. No one paid any attention at the time to the swelling on her left leg, which was assumed to have been caused by an insect bite.

A few weeks later, though, Robert James was accused of accosting a woman on the street and police began to take a greater interest in him. He was a native Alabaman, it turned out, with a taste for sado-masochism. He'd also been married five times. This in itself didn't necessarily mean much, but his third wife had also drowned – this time in the bath – a short while after they'd been married. James had collected thousands of dollars in insurance from a policy on her life – just as he was now going to do from Mary's.

By this time they'd also found out about Hope's curious purchase (and return) of two rattlesnakes, and when questioned, Hope soon broke down. He said he'd bought them for his boss, who'd intended to use them to murder his wife, but had then had to find another way.

James was arrested and brought to trial, with the snakes on display in a glass case in the courtroom. The only real witness against him was Charles Hope, who turned state's evidence in return for a lesser sentence. Hope said that Lightning and Lethal were actually the third pair of rattlers he'd bought – the other two couldn't even kill a rabbit between them. On the night in question, he'd taken them to James's bungalow in a box; then when Mary James had passed out from drink, he'd helped her husband lay her on the kitchen table and undress her. At that point he'd opened the rattlers' box enough for her left leg to be shoved in.

Though she was bitten several times, it wasn't enough; she began to come round. So James, growing impatient, took her upstairs and drowned her in the bath. They then dressed her and staged the unfortunate accident in the lily-pond, pushing her face-first into the water.

'Rattlesnake' James – as he was by now known in the newspapers – was sentenced to death. He appealed several times, but was turned down each time and he was finally executed on 1 May 1942, the last man in California to be hanged. After him came the gas-chamber era.

REVEREND JIM JONES

IT'S HARD TO know the point at which the Reverend Jim Jones went bad – the dynamics of power and its effects are hard to read. But little by little he turned from being an idealistic young pastor into a fire-and-brimstone flim-flam man – and from there it only got worse. By the end, near Port Kaituma in Guiana, he'd become a paranoid Messiah, preaching a demented millenarianism that was to kill almost a thousand men, women and children.

James Warren Jones was born in 1931 in the heart of America's Bible Belt, in Lynn, Indiana, and by the age of 12 he was already preaching impromptu street sermons to children and passers-by. When he was 18, he took a job in nearby Richmond as a hospital porter, so that he could pay his way through Indiana University as a religious-studies student. He got married to a nurse and, when he graduated, he started an outreach programme for poor blacks at an Indianapolis Methodist church.

From the outset he faced often violent opposition from racists both inside and outside his Methodist congregation. So in 1957 he bought a building and opened his own church, the People's Temple, in an Indianapolis ghetto, preaching a message of racial integration and equality. He and his wife adopted seven children, black, white and Asian and he took to describing himself as 'bi-racial,' pointing up his mother's Cherokee blood. He became, in effect, an 'honorary black,' and his style of preaching owed a lot to black holy-roller showmen like Father Divine.

In return he soon secured the undeviating loyalty of a black congregation that rapidly grew as he defied the threats and attacks of white bigots – some of which, it's been suggested, he made up. Like Divine, he became a faith-healer, putting on shows at the Temple in which the 'sick' were cured and the 'disabled' walked. Some of his church elders even began to claim that he'd raised people from the dead.

In 1963, at the height of American fears about nuclear warfare, he suddenly announced that he'd had a vision of a future holocaust in which only two places would be spared: Okiah, California, and Belo Horizonte, Brazil. (The 'vision' probably came from a 1960 magazine article.) He told his congregation to get ready by selling their houses and withdrawing their savings. Then he flew to Brazil to take a look, and on his return journey stopped over for a few days in the socialist republic of Guyana.

Brazil failed the test. So in 1965, he and 300 followers from Indianapolis settled in Redwood Valley near Okiah, California. They were hard-working, charitable and seemingly deeply religious. They took in problem children and orphans and impressed the local community enough for Jones to be appointed foreman of the county grand jury and the director of its free legal-aid services.

In 1970, Jones moved his tax-exempt People's Temple to downtown San Francisco, where his congregation's reputation as a willing and energetic army for good quickly followed him. The church's membership soon swelled to 7,500, both black and white; and the city turned over part of its welfare programme to it. Jones also carefully nurtured its public image, by making donations to the police welfare fund and awards to the press 'for outstanding journalistic contributions to peace and public enlightenment' in its name. He was even invited to President Carter's inauguration in Washington in 1976.

By 1976, though, defectors from the People's Temple were beginning to tell the press about Jones's obsession with sex: about how he preached sexual abstinence, but treated female members of the church as his harem; about how he forced grown men to confess to imagined sins of homosexuality and browbeat married couples into divorce, so that they could then be reassigned to whoever he chose. There was worse: there were public beatings of children to make them show respect – a cattleprod was even used on the most recalcitrant; and there were sinister congregation-wide rehearsals – so-called 'White Nights' – for what Jones termed 'revolutionary mass suicide.'

By the following year, pressure from the press and public censure had become so intense that Jones put into effect his escape plan. Using the money provided by his congregation, he had already bought a lease on 20,000 acres of jungle and swamp in Guyana, where a pavilion and dormitories had been built. In November 1977, he and a thousand loyal members of the congregation moved there. According to a 1978 report in the *San Francisco Chronicle*, the new community at Jonestown was surrounded by armed guards and subject to 'public beatings' and 'a threat of mass suicide.'

When California Congressman Leo Ryan read this, he made it his business to talk to the relatives of the people at Jonestown who were afraid they were being held there against their will. He then asked the federal authorities to intervene with the Guyanan government, and shortly afterwards flew to Jonestown himself with a team of newspaper and television journalists.

When they arrived at Jonestown, they found Jones holding court at the pavilion, with 1,000 American passports locked in a strongroom at his back. At first, the interviews with him and with members of the congregation went well. The armed guards were there simply 'to keep out the bandits;' and yes, Jones did have a number of mistresses, but the idea that his followers were not permitted to have sex was 'bullshit: thirty babies have been born since summer 1977.' The citizens of Jonestown still seemed fanatically devoted to their leader; the only sour note that was struck was when Ryan offered to put under his personal protection anyone who wanted to leave.

The next day, when Ryan – who had stayed in Jonestown overnight – was picked up by the reporters, they found 20 congregation-members who wanted to leave with him. There was a scuffle when one of the church elders tried to stab Ryan. So the press, Ryan and as many defectors who could get on board an earth-moving machine took off to the airstrip where their chartered plane was waiting. There they were later ambushed by Jones and his armed guards. Ryan, three journalists and two of the defectors were killed.

Back at the settlement, Jones immediately gave orders for mass suicide. Babies had cyanide squirted into their mouths with syringes. Older children drank cups of Kool-Aid laced with poison from huge vats, followed shortly by their parents. When the Guyanese army arrived at the settlement the next day, they found whole families embraced in death, and the Reverend Jim Jones with a bullet through his brain.

After the mass suicide, a white professor who'd been a member of Jones's congregation in its Okiah days said that it had been based on the idealistic Oneida community, which also allowed multiple marriages. A dark hint of this – and a reminder of what it had become – was left in a suicide note, addressed to Jones, found at the scene. It said in part:

'Dad, I can see no way out, I agree with your decision. Without you the world may not make it to Communism. . .'

TED KACZYNSKI

IT TOOK ALMOST 18 years to link loner Ted Kaczynski to the killer known only by his FBI code-name, Unabomber. By then his bombs had become more and more sophisticated and deadly – and there was a million-dollar reward on his head.

His beginnings, in Chicago, had been modest. In May 1978, a package carrying the return address of a professor at Northwestern University's Technological Institute exploded while being opened by campus police. Shortly afterwards, a Northwestern graduate student opened an unaddressed cigar box he found and also sustained minor injuries. Bomb number three was found in the hold of an American Airlines plane outward bound from O'Hare Airport after its cabin had filled with smoke; bomb number four was in a parcel addressed to the president of United Airlines in Lake Forest. All were relatively crude affairs – though the airline bomb had been triggered to go off at a certain altitude – and did little damage.

There was then a lull of more than a year. But another bomb was found – and successfully defused – in a business classroom at the University of Utah in Salt Lake City in May 1982; it was followed a year later by a parcel bomb apparently intended for a professor of electrical engineering at Brigham Young. Less than two months later, another electrical-engineering professor, this time at the University of California at Berkeley, picked up a can of some kind in the faculty lounge and was seriously injured when it exploded.

By now the FBI had a tentative idea of who the bomber might be: an educated, intelligent white male, possibly an academic, from the Chicago area, with a grudge against authority in general and universities in particular. It was also clear that he was learning on the job, for his bombs were getting more and more sophisticated. Then, though, for three years the trail went cold, nothing happened – until suddenly bombs started appearing again on the West Coast, in Salt Lake City, Utah, and Ann Arbor, Michigan, in 1985.

The targets, this time, were computers, behaviour-modification and, once again, aircraft. Bombs were hand-delivered to two computer stores and a computer room at Berkeley and sent by post to the Boeing Aircraft Fabrication Division and a psychology professor in Ann Arbor. Four people were injured, two of them seriously; one of the computer-store operators was killed.

Once again there was a lull, this time for six years. Then, one after another, a geneticist at the University of California, a computer scientist at Yale and a vice-president of the Young & Rubicam advertising agency in New York were all hit. In a long, rambling letter sent to the *New York Times* a few months later, the Unabomber railed against computers and genetic engineering and claimed that the adman – who'd been killed instantly –

had been part of a conspiracy, involved in 'manipulating people's attitudes.' On the day the letter was received, he struck again: a parcel bomb killed the president of the California Forestry Association in Sacramento.

This immediately suggested that the Unabomber was now playing games. For the surname and second name of two of his early victims had been Wood; the bombs had mostly been found in wooden containers. And, sure enough, when another letter was subsequently sent, this time to the *San Francisco Chronicle*, it carried as a return address 'Frederick Benjamin Isaac [FBI] Wood, 549 Wood Street, Woodlake, California'.

By this time the Unabomber was in regular communication with the *New York Times* and the *Washington Post*; he finally announced to both newspapers that he would give up his bombing campaign if they published in full a 35,000-word manifesto he'd written, spelling out his hatred of modern, technology-driven America. They agreed and it was read by a social worker in upstate New York called David Kaczynski.

Kaczynski was struck by the similarity of certain phrases in the manifesto to those written by his brother Theodore, a failed academic living in a tiny cabin without electricity outside Lincoln, Montana. After taking advice from friends, he finally went to the FBI with his suspicions. The cabin outside Lincoln was raided, and along with Ted Kaczynski, bomb-making equipment and early drafts of the manifesto were found.

Kaczynski was a 55-year-old Harvard graduate who'd done post-graduate work at Ann Arbor, and had faced a fast-track career as professor of mathematics at Berkeley. Then, unable to cope with the pressures of life, he'd simply dropped out. He started sending and laying bombs for 'personal revenge,' he wrote in his diary in 1971, because he was 'superior to most of the rest of the human race' and yet had been subject to 'rejections, humiliations and other painful influences.' He was sentenced to life imprisonment without the possibility of parole on 22 January 1998.

ED KEMPER

ED KEMPER, WHOSE parents separated when he was seven, grew up troubled and sadistic. He tortured animals; he once cut the hands and feet off his sister's doll. But with people he was painfully shy. When his sister teased him about secretly wanting to kiss his teacher, he said:

'If I kissed her, I'd have to kill her first.'

And this is precisely what the adult Ed Kemper – 6 feet 9 inches tall and weighing almost 300 pounds – did. But first there was a teenage prelude. For in 1962, when he was 13, he ran away from the mother he hated to join his father – and his father promptly sent him back. Unwanted by either, he was despatched to live with his grandparents on a ranch in California and two years later he shot them both dead. He was, in other words, a serial time-bomb which had already begun to go off.

After five years in a hospital for the criminally insane, he was released into the care of his mother, who was then living in Santa Cruz. It was a bitter household. But Kemper got a job as a labourer, and finally bought himself a car. He began to pick up hitch-hikers.

On 7 May 1972, he picked up two women students from Fresno State College, Anita Luchese and Mary Anne Pesce, held them at gunpoint and

Ed Kemper picked up hitchhikers before brutally slaying them.

drove them out to a wooded canyon. He stabbed them both to death and raped their corpses, before taking the bodies back home in the trunk of his car. Upstairs in his room, he took off their heads with his hunting knife – nicknamed 'the General' – had sex again with their corpses and then dissected them. He buried what was left in the mountains.

Four months later, on 14 September, he picked up a 15-year-old high-school student, and again drove her, at gunpoint, up into the mountains. He taped her mouth and suffocated her by sticking his fingers up her nostrils. Then, as earlier, he raped her, took her home and cut off her head, had sex with her again and dismembered her. His mother noticed nothing unusual as he took her remains out to the car in garbage bags for disposal.

After another four-month interval, in January 1973, he struck again, and again his victim was a student, this time at Cabrillo College. Claudia Schall was shot on a quiet road near Freedom, California, dumped into the trunk and then hidden in a closet in Kemper's bedroom. The following morning, after his mother had gone to work, he violated her corpse and then cut it up with an axe in the shower. Parts of her body were later discovered and identified after he'd thrown them off cliffs at Carmel.

A month later, he picked up two more students after a particularly vicious row with his mother. He shot them both in the head and drove their bodies back, only to find that his mother was still home. Unable to wait, he decapitated both bodies in the trunk; the next morning, after his mother had gone, he took the headless corpses upstairs and had sex with at least one of them. Then, after cutting off the hands of one of the students and getting rid of both heads, he dumped the bodies in Eden Canyon, Alameda – where they were found nine days later.

Kemper's killings can be seen to have been caused – at least in part – by his hatred of his mother; and on Easter Day, 1973, he went to the source: he killed her in her bedroom with a hammer and cut off her head with 'the General'. Then he invited one of her woman friends, Sara Hallett, to dinner, knocked her unconscious, strangled, decapitated and had sex with her. The next morning, after sleeping in his mother's bed, he took the money from Mrs Hallett's handbag and drove off in her car, expecting that the police would be after him.

In the end, when nothing happened, he gave himself up, after finally persuading the police that he really was the so-called 'Co-Ed Killer'. Now there could be no doubt. He'd cut out his mother's larynx, he said, and tossed it into the garbage,

'because it seemed appropriate after she had bitched me so much.'

Kemper was found sane and despite his request to be executed, was sentenced to life imprisonment without the possibility of parole.

MEYER LANSKY

MEYER LANSKY, BORN Maier Suchowjansky in Grodno, Poland, is the most shadowy and indistinct of all the great American Mafia bosses of the 20 century. But it was he more than anyone else who was responsible for creating the structure and outreach of the modern Mafia – first by master-minding the alliance between New York's Italian and Jewish mobs that created the central commission, the Syndicate, and then by expanding the Syndicate's reach and influence across the United States and beyond. It was he, the grand strategist, who moved the Mafia's money and power into Las Vegas, movies and legitimate businesses all across the country. He said in the 1970s – and only he perhaps knew:

'We're bigger than US Steel.'

In about 1918, 16-year-old Lansky arrived in New York and seems to have taken a job as an engineering apprentice. But he was soon part of the rough-and-tumble of the Lower East Side's streets, running with the Jewish gangs and fighting for both territory and survival. The turning point came when he met and outfaced another tough street kid called Charlie Luciano, who took him under his wing. Many of the underground rackets in the city were then run by Jewish gangsters, and Lansky became in time Luciano's bridge to their operations and muscle. 'We had a kind of instant understanding,' Luciano later said.

'It may sound crazy, but if anyone wants to use the expression "blood brothers", then surely Meyer and I were like that.'

Both Luciano and Lansky in due course made it to the big time: they went to work for the visionary Arnold Rothstein, the first great bootlegger of the Prohibition era – and the first man, it's said, to recognize the potential of dope. Rothstein – Lansky is said to have met him at a bar mitzvah – taught both men a good deal about style, and gave Lansky his first taste of what was later to become his main operation: casino gambling.

Rothstein was assassinated in 1928 and left the field open to the fastest learners among his apprentices, Luciano and Lansky. They largely sat out the score-settling wars that followed. But then, in 1931, Lansky organized the Jewish hit-men who disposed of the first self-styled *Capo di Tutti Capi*, Salvatore Maranzano, who'd set himself up as the ultimate authority over what came to be known as 'the five families.' He and Luciano took over Maranzano's five-family structure, but instead of appointing a boss of all bosses, they created a board of directors, the Syndicate, backed by the enforcement arm of Murder Incorporated. Both sat on the Syndicate board, and met every day they could, it's said, for breakfast at a delicatessen on Delancey Street. Luciano and Lansky: they were the real power.

They moved the Mafia into dope – it's said that Lansky himself got hooked on heroin after his son was born crippled, and then did cold turkey in a hide-out in Massachusetts, watched over by a hood called Vincent 'Jimmy Blue Eyes' Alo, ever after a close friend. They became the ultimate authority in policy and peace, ruling Mafia activity nationwide. But then in 1936, 'Lucky' Luciano was tried on a trumped-up charge of prostitution and sentenced to 30 to 50 years in jail. After that, Lansky more and more took to the shadows, living apparently quietly in a tract house in Miami, as he moved the Mafia into gambling operations in Las Vegas, the Bahamas and Cuba.

In 1970, after hearing that he faced tax-evasion charges, Lansky, by now 68, fled to a hotel he owned in Tel Aviv, before being extradited, by order of the Israeli Supreme Court, back to the US. In the end, he was acquitted, and in the late-70s and early-80s, he could be seen walking his dog along Miami's Collins Avenue or else having a meal in a diner with his old friend 'Jimmy Blue Eyes.' He died from a heart attack in 1983, at the age of 81.

NATHAN LEOPOLD AND RICHARD LOEB

IT WAS CALLED at the time the 'crime of the century', a 'superman' murder. But in reality the 1924 killing of Bobbie Franks by two young University of Chicago students, Nathan Leopold and Richard Loeb, was both senseless and lazy. Far from being the 'perfect' murder, a secret demonstration of how much 'better' and 'less bourgeois' they were than their friends and relatives, it only proved that even intellectuals can be supremely cack-handed.

Fourteen-year-old Bobbie, the son of a millionaire, was abducted outside his school on 21 May 1924 and soon afterwards his mother received a call saying that he'd been kidnapped and that a ransom note would arrive through the post. The next day it came, demanding $10,000. But before anything could be done, the police announced that they'd found a body that matched Bobbie's description. It had been discovered by maintenance men – strangled and with a fractured skull – in a culvert near the railway. Nearby lay a pair of horn-rimmed spectacles.

It took a week for the spectacles to be traced to a rich 19-year-old law student and amateur ornithologist called Nathan Leopold. Leopold immediately agreed that they were indeed his, and he claimed that he must have dropped them while bird-watching in the area some time before. But the spectacles showed no sign of having been left outside for long and when Leopold was asked what he'd been doing on the afternoon of 21 May, all he could come up with was that he'd been with his friend, fellow student Richard Loeb, and two girls called Mae and Edna. Loeb soon corroborated this, but neither man could give any sort of description by which the two girls could be traced. Besides, Leopold's typewriter, when tested, was found to be exactly the same model as the one which had written the ransom note.

It was, oddly, Richard Loeb – easily the more assured and dominant of the two men – who first confessed under questioning. But he was soon followed by Leopold, whose younger brother, it turned out, had been a friend of Bobbie Franks. The 14-year-old had been chosen as their victim, it transpired, not because of any particular enmity, but for a much simpler reason: he'd be easy to get into their car.

Two months after the killing, defended by famous lawyer Clarence Darrow, they came to trial. Darrow did his best, claiming that both his clients were mentally ill, either paranoiac (in Leopold's case) or schizophrenic (in Loeb's). This defence probably saved their lives, but they were imprisoned for life for Bobbie's murder, and given a further 99 years' sentence for his kidnapping. Twelve years later, Loeb was killed by a fellow inmate. But Leopold, who'd been throughout his term a model prisoner, was finally released in 1958. He moved to Puerto Rico, got married, and died in 1971 at the age of 66.

LOUIS LEPKE

LOUIS LEPKE, the boss of the Jewish arm of Murder Incorporated, is the only American Mafia chieftain to have been executed. After two years hiding out in Brooklyn, he gave himself up to the FBI, persuaded into doing so, it's said, by Albert Anastasia. He, 'Lucky' Luciano and the other members of the Syndicate wanted him dead.

Lepke, short for 'Lepkele' or 'Little Louis', was born Louis Buchalter in Williamsburg, Brooklyn, in 1897. His father, the owner of a hardware store on the Lower East Side, died of a heart attack when he was 13, and his mother moved soon afterwards to Colorado. Little Louis, then, came of age in the streets. He hung out with hoodlums, and was soon in trouble with the law. He was sent out of town to live with his uncle in Connecticut, and then to a reformatory, from where he soon graduated, around the time of his 21st birthday, first to New York's Tombs prison, and then to Sing Sing, where he acquired the nickname 'Judge Louis'.

Back on the streets again in 1923, he went into the protection business with an old pal, Joseph 'Gurrah' Shapiro – they were known as 'the Gorilla Boys' and specialized in bakeries. But they didn't hit the big time until they went to work for Arnold Rothstein, who dealt large in liquor and drugs. Soon they were moving into the union rackets, backing the workers against the bosses with goon squads, and then taking over from both. They started out in this with a real expert, 'Little Augie' Orgen, as their principal mentor. But by 1927, Orgen simply stood in their way. So on 15 October, they gunned him down in front of his clubhouse and by the beginning of the '30s they ruled the labour roost: they controlled painters, truckers and motion-picture operators; they were expanding their drugs business; and they still took in $1.5 million a year from bakeries. They were now known, not as 'the Gorilla Boys', but 'the Gold Dust Twins'.

In 1933, with the setting up of the Syndicate, Lepke became a board-director and one of the founding members of Murder Incorporated, its enforcement arm of contract-killers, among whom was a Brooklyn thug called Abraham 'Kid Twist' Reles. That same year, though, Lepke was indicted by a federal grand jury for violation of anti-trust laws. And though he ultimately beat the rap on this one, the Feds began closing in with narcotics charges, and the Brooklyn DA's office with an investigation into racketeering. In the summer of 1937, he – along with 'Gurrah' Shapiro – went on the lam; he soon became the most wanted man in US history.

He did his best from hiding to silence the potential witnesses against him, but the heat on the streets became too great and, in August 1940, he gave himself up, with the understanding that he'd face federal narcotics charges rather than a state indictment for murder. He was sentenced to 14 years and shipped to the penitentiary at Leavenworth, Kansas.

Then, though, Abe Reles, 'Kid Twist,' one of the executioners he'd hired in the old days, began to sing. For six months Reles was held at a hotel in Coney Island as he gave evidence at trial after trial. On 12 November 1941, his body was found – apparently he'd jumped from a sixth story window – but it was too late for Louis Lepke. For Reles had already appeared before a grand-jury hearing to give evidence against him, evidence that could be – and was – used in court.

Louis Lepke and two of his lieutenants, Mendy Weiss and Louis Capone, were tried for murder and condemned to death. They went to the electric chair in Sing Sing prison on 4 March 1944. The murder of Reles – which got Albert Anastasia and Bugsy Siegel off the hook – was probably arranged by Frank Costello.

TIMOTHY MCVEIGH

IT WAS ONE of the most devastating crimes in all US history. A hundred and sixty-eight people were killed and more than 500 wounded, among them twenty-five children under 5. So on 19 April 1995, when the dust finally settled on what remained of the Alfred P. Murrah Federal Building in Oklahoma City, it was taken for granted that its bombing had been the work of international terrorists. It wasn't – as those who recognized the symbolism of the date soon realized. For 19 April was Patriots Day, the anniversary of the Revolutionary War battle of Concord. It was also the second anniversary of the fiery and bloody end of David Koresh's Branch Davidian sect at Waco, Texas. The bomber wasn't Arab at all, but American: a 27-year-old ex-soldier from Pendleton, New York, called Timothy McVeigh.

McVeigh had been resourceful enough in gathering the materials that made up his huge bomb: a mixture of fuel oil, ammonium nitrate and fertilizer. But he was careless and stupid with everything else. For within an hour and a half of its explosion, he was stopped by a state trooper 75 miles away for driving his getaway car without a licence plate. The trooper then noticed a gun in the car and arrested him. He was taken to jail in Perry, Oklahoma.

It's possible that he still might have got away – and disappeared – if the identification number of the 20-foot-long Ryder truck he'd armed with the bomb hadn't been recovered. The FBI traced it to a hire-firm in Kansas where they were able to get a description of the man who'd rented it. Transformed into a sketch by FBI artists, this description was soon recognized by the owner of a motel in Junction City, who was able to pass on the name in his register – incredibly enough, McVeigh's own. From that point on, it was plain sailing. The name Timothy J. McVeigh was logged into the National Crime Information computer, which revealed that he was under arrest in Perry on an unrelated charge. From there it just took a phone call.

The question people came to ask, then, was no longer 'Who?', but 'Why?' And the answer travelled deep into the paranoid, poor-white underbelly of American power.

Timothy McVeigh was a classic case of the angry, antisocial loser who blamed his own inadequacies on a conspiracy designed to keep him down. He came from a broken family; lived with a father who didn't much care for him; and failed to be remembered at school. He enrolled for a while at the local community college, but soon dropped out for a menial job at Burger King. It was only when he applied for a gun licence and moved to Buffalo, New York, to become an armoured-car guard there, that he finally found what seemed to be the only passion he ever really had in his life: guns.

That he then joined the army seems now, in retrospect, a natural enough progression. He trained at Fort Benning, Georgia, where he met two equally needy men who later became co-conspirators in his bombing: Terry Nichols and Michael Fortier. It was they, perhaps, who introduced him to William L. Pierce's fiercely anti-Semitic *The Turner Diaries*, one of the bibles of American white supremacists. The story concerns a soldier in an underground army who, in response to efforts to ban private ownership of guns, builds a fertilizer-and-fuel oil bomb packed into a truck to blow up the FBI building in Washington...

McVeigh became a gunner and served with some distinction in the Gulf War. But when he failed in later tests to become a member of Special Forces, he left the army and became a drifter. He stayed for a while with his two army buddies, Fortier and Nichols, in Arizona and Michigan respectively. But mostly he lived out of his car, collecting gun magazines, attending gun fairs and railing against blacks, Jews and the hated Federal government. In 1993, he even went to Waco, Texas, during the Branch Davidian sect's initial standoff with the Bureau of Alcohol, Tobacco and Firearms. He sold bumper stickers there which denounced the government for trying to take away the nation's guns.

What subsequently happened at Waco was the trigger that set off the Oklahoma bomb. For McVeigh now determinedly entered what he called the 'action stage.' Together with Fortier and Nichols – and with

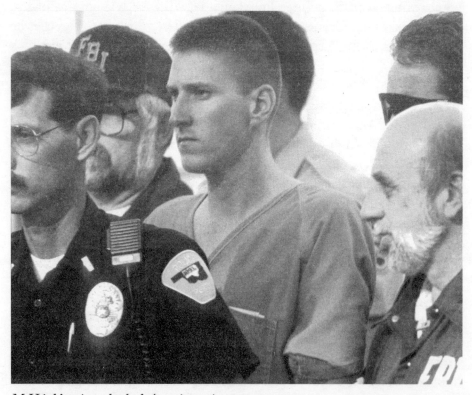

McVeigh's crime shocked America to its core.

The Turner Diaries as a guide – he mapped out his plan: to use a massive bomb against the federal government as revenge, warning and call to arms. Though Fortier, and later Nichols, both dropped out of a final commitment, he didn't care. He drove the Ryder truck to Oklahoma City and then left a sign on it saying that it had a flat battery, so that it wouldn't be towed away.

When arrested in Parry, McVeigh – true to form – insisted on calling himself a prisoner of war. He was tried and sentenced to death.

CHARLES MANSON

FROM THE AGE of nine until he was 32, Charles Manson, born illegitimate, spent almost all his life in institutions, though he did spend enough time on the outside to be sent down for armed robbery (at 13), homosexual rape (at 17) and car stealing, fraud and pimping (at 23). In prison for this last set of offences, he became, by an odd coincidence, the protégé of another killer, Alvin Karpis of the notorious Barker Gang, who taught him the guitar well enough for him to be able to boast later:

'I could be bigger than the Beatles.'

In a way, of course, Manson was. For, let out of prison in 1967, the year of 'the summer of love,' he became the most hated and vilified figure in America, a symbol of everything that had gone wrong in the '60s.

Emerging from San Pedro prison with little more than a beard, a guitar and a line in mystic hocus-pocus, Manson was soon playing hippie Jesus on the streets of San Francisco's Haight-Ashbury to a group of adoring disciples – most of them middle-class drop-outs who lived on a diet of hallucinogenic drugs and acted out their fantasies in sex orgies. It wasn't long, though, before he decided his ambitions were too big for San Francisco. So he took his 'Family' south, picking up new acolytes on the way, and settled in the grounds of the Spiral Staircase club in Los Angeles, where he began to attract the attention of the wilder fringes of the Hollywood party scene: musicians, agents and actors looking for kicks or black magic – or the next big thing.

Manson's vision, though, by this time was becoming darker, more apocalyptic, and by the time he moved the 'Family' to the Spahn Movie

Ranch 30 miles from the city, he was no longer interested in merely sex, drugs and adoration. He believed that there would soon be a nuclear day of reckoning, called Helter Skelter. He drew up a death list of people he envied or wanted revenge on ('pigs' like Warren Beattie and Julie Christie) and he became obsessed with the idea of a dune-buggy-riding army of survivalists which would escape into the Mojave Desert.

To set up this army – and its transport – he, of course, needed money.

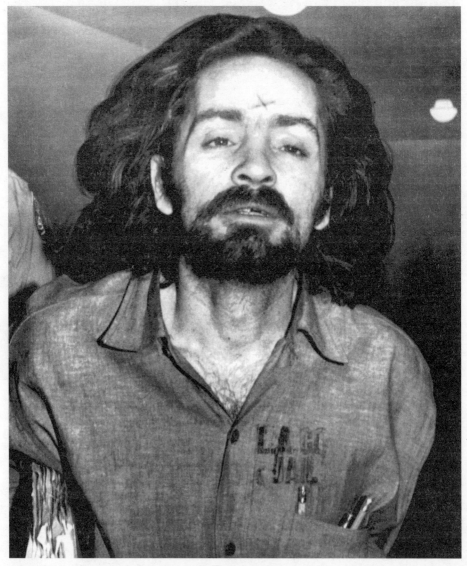

Manson has been denied parole a total of 12 times.

So, like a latter-day Fagin, he set his 'Family' to crime: drug-dealing, theft, robbery, credit-card fraud, prostitution and eventually murder. First, a drug-dealer, a bit-part actor and a musician were killed on his orders; and then, when some of his 'Family' were arrested on other charges, he announced Helter Skelter day.

That night, 8 August 1969, four of his demented disciples invaded the house of director Roman Polanski and murdered five people, including his pregnant wife Sharon Tate. Before they left, they used Tate's blood to daub the word PIG on the front door.

When he later heard the names of the victims, Manson – who'd chosen the house only because one of the people on his death-list had once lived there – was delighted. As Hollywood panicked, he led the next murderous raid himself, selecting a house for no other reason than that it was next-door to someone he disliked. This time a 44-year old supermarket president called Leno LaBianca and his wife Rosemary were stabbed in a frenzy, and their blood used to write DEATH TO PIGS, RISE and HEALTER [sic] SKELTER on the walls. The word WAR was carved onto Mr LaBianca's stomach.

The two cases of multiple murder were investigated by different law-enforcement agencies and at first no connections were made. Manson and members of the 'Family' were arrested, but on other charges, and were eventually released. But then one of Manson's female acolytes confessed to a cell-mate that she'd been involved in the murders and eventually he and other members of the 'Family,' two of whom later turned state's evidence, were picked up.

The trial of Manson and three of his female acolytes – others were tried elsewhere – lasted nine months, and was not without sensation. When Manson appeared in the dock one day with a cross carved with a razor-blade onto his forehead, the three girls soon burned the same mark onto theirs. On another occasion 5 foot 2 inches-tall Manson jumped 10 feet across the counsel table to attack the judge, who afterwards took to carrying a revolver.

In the end all four were sentenced to death, but were spared execution when the California Supreme Court voted to abolish the death penalty in 1972. Manson was denied parole on no fewer than twelve occasions, and died in November 2017.

WALTER LEROY MOODY

WALTER LEROY (ROY) MOODY JR was a bomb-maker: an intelligent, manipulative man with a sense of failure and a strong grudge against the world. The trouble was, he was also a perfectionist, with a perfectionist's distaste for the ordinary. His bombs were carefully designed – at some danger to himself – to do as much damage as possible, and once he'd hit on the best way of ensuring this, he saw no reason to change it at all. Unfortunately for him, then, every calling card he sent out in his campaign for revenge had a signature – a signature the police had already seen.

Moody's first calling card arrived on the afternoon of 16 December 1989 at a house near Birmingham, Alabama, when Robert Vance, a US Circuit Court of Appeals judge, sitting with his wife at the kitchen table, opened a package. An explosion ripped into him and killed him. His wife, sitting at the opposite end of the table, was hurled back onto the floor and hit by a nail, added as shrapnel, which tore through her liver and one of her lungs.

US marshals across the country were immediately warned of a possible continuing parcel-bomb attack on people in the judiciary. Extreme care, they were told, was to be taken with any suspicious packages. Two days later, sure enough, another bomb was found, this time by a security officer using an X-ray machine to vet mail at the 11th Circuit Court of Appeals in Atlanta, where Judge Vance had served.

That was not the only one of Moody's calling cards, though, that was delivered that day. For that afternoon, in Savannah, Georgia, when black attorney Robert Robinson opened his mail at his desk, another explosion ripped through him, blowing off his arm and leaving pieces of his bone and flesh painted on the walls. The same would have happened, no doubt, to the NAACP branch-president in Jacksonville, Mississippi, if she hadn't had trouble with her car. By the time she got into her office the following day, she'd heard the word about the other package-bombs and, just to be safe, called in the sheriff's office.

Robinson had by that time died in hospital. But the FBI and the Bureau of Alcohol, Tobacco and Firearms had already, with the help of the Atlanta police, dismantled the bomb sent to the 11th Circuit Court. Using this bomb as a template, they were now able relatively easily to take apart the Jacksonville one. Both were pipe bombs, but they had curious features:

nails had been attached to the pipe by rubber bands, and the ends of the pipes had been closed off with welded metal plates. A bolted rod had also been passed through the pipe to strengthen it. None of the veteran bomb-experts had seen a configuration like this before.

The first assumption of detectives was the bombs were part of a campaign by a white supremacist group. For a tear-gas grenade had exploded in a package at an NAACP office in Atlanta the previous August, and at around the same time a letter titled 'Declaration of War' had begun showing up at television stations, including one in Atlanta, railing against the 11th Circuit Court of Appeal – which, among other things, tried civil rights cases – and threatening poison-gas attacks. Another letter had been received by an Atlanta TV anchorwoman, denouncing and threatening with death US judges and black leaders for failing 'to prevent black men from raping white women.'

When no supremacist group claimed responsibility, though, the FBI began to change its mind – to believe that the bombings had been the work of a white middle-aged loner with a grudge. And this was when local bomb-squad veterans began to remember that they'd seen a bomb constructed like this before.

In 1972 a woman called Hazel Moody had opened a package she thought to contain model-airplane parts for her husband. It exploded in her face, leaving her with first- and second-degree burns, a destroyed hand and a badly damaged eye. But the package had actually been addressed to a car dealership which had recently repossessed her and her husband's car. It was meant to be posted. Her husband, Roy Moody, had been responsible, and had been jailed for five years, but was still, apparently, appealing his sentence, most recently – and unsuccessfully – in the 11th Circuit Court of Appeals.

Moody fitted the profile of a middle-aged white loner with a grudge exactly. By now in his mid-fifties, he'd trained in both neurosurgery and the law, but he'd failed at the first and couldn't practise the second because of the bomb conviction. He was manipulative and potentially dangerous – a 1983 trial of Moody for attempted murder had ended in a hung jury. He was soon arrested.

The trouble was that the FBI still had nothing but strong circumstantial evidence against him. It wasn't until his second wife, whom he'd brutalized, agreed to testify that the murder case could finally be made. She told the court in detail about the locked bedroom she was never allowed to enter;

about how she was sent off in disguise to distant stores to make purchases of bomb ingredients for him; and how she mailed packages for him, packages she wasn't allowed to look at. On the testimony of his battered wife, Roy Moody, already serving life without parole on federal charges relating to the bombings, was finally sentenced to the electric chair in Alabama for the murder of Judge Vance in 1997.

HERMAN MUDGETT, AKA H.H. HOLMES

HERMAN MUDGETT, ALIAS H.H. Holmes, alias H.M. Howard, was an insurance swindler and a bigamist. But he was also one of the most prolific serial killers in American history. He liked to handle dead bodies.

He was born in Gilmanton, New Hampshire, in May 1860 and certainly trained as a doctor, perhaps in New York. But he first came to fame in Chicago where, after deserting his wife and using the name H.H. Holmes, he took over a pharmacy from its proprietor, a Mrs Holden, who'd been employing him until she disappeared. Business soon thrived and in 1890, having married again, he started building a battlemented house-cum-hotel which became known as Holmes's Castle.

Holmes's Castle was no ordinary establishment, though. For concealed within it was a maze of shafts and chutes and hidden passages. There were also secret airtight rooms which could be filled with piped gas via a control-switch in the office, and a basement which contained huge vats. Only Mudgett himself knew the Castle's overall design, for he hired different builders to work, in isolation from each other, on their own small sections of the building.

It was completed and opened in time for the Chicago Exposition of 1893, which brought huge numbers of visitors to the city, many of them young women on their own. Having already, allegedly, got rid of several of his mistresses, Mudgett now had a machine that could deliver his female victims to death with maximum efficiency. After luring them from their rooms and attempting to seduce them, he would place them in one of the shafts giving onto a secret cell, and there gas them to death behind airtight glass panels. Then a chute would deliver their bodies to the basement, where he could dissect them at will, before tossing what remained of them into vats containing acid and lime.

In the year of the Exposition, Mudgett killed tens, perhaps hundreds, of young women and girls. But finally he got greedy. For among his victims were two rich sisters from Texas and he decided, rather than stay in Chicago, to go after their fortune. So he set fire to the Castle, and claimed the insurance; then, when the insurance company refused to pay and the police announced an investigation into the causes of the fire, he fled the city southward.

Once in Texas he ingratiated himself with the two sisters' relatives, and did his best to swindle them out of a $60,000 legacy. When this failed – and with the law close behind him – he took off on a stolen horse. He was finally caught in Missouri, using the name H.M. Howard, and already charged there with fraud. But with the help of a crooked lawyer he was granted bail – and again he escaped.

He next appeared in Philadelphia, where a man called Benjamin Pitezel had been his associate, it later emerged, in a number of insurance scams. Pitezel, whose life had been insured for $10,000, was soon blown up in what seemed to be an accident; Mudgett was one of those who identified his body. He had, of course, killed Pitezel himself and when the insurance company paid the $10,000 to Pitezel's wife, he disappeared with her and her three children. The children didn't last long, though: they were later found dead, two of them in a basement in Toronto, Canada, and one in a chimney in Irvington.

Mudgett was finally arrested, along with his mistress, in Boston in mid-1885. He'd been tracked down by detectives who were after him not, oddly, for the crimes he'd committed in Chicago or Philadelphia, but for jumping bail in Missouri and horse-stealing in Texas – at that time a capital offence. The Philadelphia courts, however, had first crack at him, for the murder of Benjamin Pitezel, to which he'd readily confessed. Evidence in the trial, though, was also given by a Chicago mechanic, who told how he'd been hired by Mudgett to strip the flesh off three corpses at his Castle. It was only after this that the Chicago police began seriously to investigate that long-ago fire and found the secrets Holmes's Castle had contained

Herman Mudgett was hanged at Philadelphia's Moyamensing Prison on 7 May 1896. In 2003, 107 years later, the Hollywood trade papers announced that two separate films about his criminal career were to be made.

BONNIE PARKER AND CLYDE BARROW

THE RELATIONSHIP BETWEEN Bonnie Parker and farmer's boy Clyde Barrow didn't get off to a good start. The first time 21-year-old Clyde came calling at her house in Cement City, Texas, he was arrested for burglary and car theft – he later got two years in jail. Nineteen-year-old Bonnie, though, was no stranger to this kind of trouble – the man she'd married three years before had been sent down for 99 years for murder. So she knew just what to do. She smuggled a gun in to Clyde as he languished behind bars, and he duly made his escape. Trouble was, he was recaptured in a matter of days after holding up a railroad office. This time he got 14 years.

True love, though – as it's said – conquers all and Clyde was soon out, though this time on crutches: he'd persuaded a fellow prisoner to cut off two of his toes with an axe. To please Bonnie's devout Baptist mother, he then tried to go straight. He took a job in Massachusetts, but it didn't last long – he pined too much for home. He returned to West Dallas, and three days later they were both gone, off to gather material for the poem Bonnie later wrote, *The Story of Bonnie and Clyde*.

With three men along for the ride, Bonnie and Clyde robbed and hijacked their way across Texas. Bonnie was picked up on suspicion of car theft, so the first three murders the gang was responsible for were committed without her. First, in April 1932, they shot a jeweller in Hillsboro, Texas, for just $40, and then, just for kicks, a sheriff and his deputy as they stood minding their business outside a dance-hall.

They never took big money: the biggest haul they ever came up with was $3,500 from a filling-station in Grand Prairie – and it didn't take them long to blow that on tour of the best hotels and restaurants they could find. The rest was penny-ante stuff, and increasingly they killed for it. Bonnie gunned down a Texas butcher for small change; and even 16-year-old William James got in on the act: he shot to death the owner of a car he was caught stealing.

By now they were notorious and in April 1933 in Missouri, joined by Clyde's brother Buck and sister-in-law Blanche, they had to shoot their way out of the apartment building they were staying in, killing two policemen in the process. Later, after a car accident in which Bonnie was badly burned, the farmer who took them in became suspicious and called the

Bonnie and Clyde are probably the most famous criminal couple in history.

police; again they had to come out firing. Finally, in July, while resting up in a tourist-camp in Missouri – and once again surrounded – they fought yet another running battle in which Buck was killed and Blanche taken. Only Bonnie and Clyde got away.

In her poem, Bonnie predicted that she and Clyde would die, and after another ten months of running they did. Their V-8 sedan was ambushed by six heavily armed policemen who pumped 87 bullets into it. They hadn't stood a chance.

When the remains of 23-year-old Bonnie and 25-year-old Clyde were buried in Dallas, huge crowds flocked to their funeral. The flowers were snatched from the top of their coffins and taken as souvenirs. Long before Arthur Penn's rosy-eyed film version of the brief career of the two young killers, they were already stars.

RICHARD RAMIREZ

THE PROBLEM WITH Richard Ramirez was the pattern of his crimes – or rather the absence of pattern. For almost all serial murderers fixate on a particular type of prey: prostitutes, say; young women; children; adolescent boys or girls – and Ramirez was an equal-opportunity killer. His 13 victims included men and women, whites and blacks; they ranged in age from 30 to 83. All they had in common was that they died in their homes at the hands of the so-called 'Night Stalker'.

Ramirez, a high-school dropout and loner, was 22 by the time he got to California from his native Texas in 1982, and by then he'd already had two arrests for drug possession. In Texas, it had been mostly marijuana and glue-sniffing, but in Los Angeles, he began shooting up cocaine and stealing from cars and houses to feed his habit. He slept wherever he found himself; he lived out of a back-pack; and ate junk food to stay alive. Pretty soon his teeth were rotting.

He did one stint in jail and it may have been this that in 1984 pushed him over the edge into murder, into making sure that 79-year-old Jennie Vincow, whose house he'd broken into, would never live to finger him. He raped and almost decapitated her and once he'd done that, he seemed to get a taste for murder. He slipped at night into people's houses and variously ripped off, raped or killed whoever he happened to find there, depending, it seemed, on his mood. In addition to the 13 murders and 30 felonies he was eventually charged with, he's thought to have racked up at least three more murders and any number of sexual assaults, some of them on young children.

He was caught, almost prosaically, by technology in the end. For three minutes after a new state-wide computerized fingerprint system was set up in Sacramento, Los Angeles police sent through a print found in a stolen car linked to 'the Night Stalker.' The system quickly came up with a match: Richard Ramirez. He was arrested two days later.

His trial dragged on for four years, largely because of Ramirez's disruptive behaviour. In continual court outbursts and long tirades, he kept referring to his worship of the devil. On at least one occasion he appeared

There seemed to be no pattern to the victims Ramirez singled out.

in court with a so-called satanic pentagram drawn on his palm. The jury was unimpressed: in November 1989, he was sentenced to death, and sent to San Quentin Prison's Death Row.

GARY RIDGWAY

ON 15 JULY 1982, two boys riding their bicycles around Kent, Washington, peered into the waters of the picturesque Green River. There, caught on a snag, was the body of a woman, naked but for a pair of jeans wrapped tightly around her neck. It was the body of 16-year-old Wendy Lee Coffield, the first official victim of a terrifying sexual predator who became known as the Green River Killer.

Gary Ridgway was born in 1949 in Salt Lake City, Utah. The middle child in a family of three boys, he struggled at school and his childhood was marked by his domineering and violent mother. At the age of 13, he was still a bed-wetter. His father drove a city bus and regularly voiced his vehement disapproval of the prostitutes who worked along his route – an attitude his son Gary was also to adopt.

By 1980, Ridgway had already clocked up two failed marriages and had begun to frequent prostitutes along the very strip his father used to drive. He was arrested on soliciting charges on a number of occasions, and was once accused of having tried to choke a prostitute.

In July and August 1982, five females aged between 16 and 31 were found in or near the mouth of the Green River. Most were prostitutes; all had been raped and strangled to death. The police wasted no time in linking the deaths and pronouncing them the work of a serial killer. By April 1983, the body count had risen to 20.

That summer, a dozen or so more women disappeared. Under mounting pressure, and inundated with tips, the police team solicited advice from all quarters, including serial killer Ted Bundy, who from his prison cell helped to form a profile of the Green River Killer.

It was all to no avail. Months, then years, passed, with more women meeting brutal deaths. Ridgway, one of numerous individuals of interest to the police, was twice given polygraph tests, in 1984 and 1986. He passed both. In 1987, his house was searched and a DNA sample taken. After police searched his locker at work, co-workers joked that he was 'Green

River Gary'. No one gave any serious thought to the notion that he might be the serial killer.

By 1986, the killing seemed to have stopped. Bodies were still being found, but the victims had died several years earlier. By 1991, the police unit investigating the case had been reduced to a single person. The case was all but dormant. But new DNA testing methods led to a breakthrough in 2001. A connection was made between semen found on the bodies of several of the victims, and the DNA taken from Ridgway in 1987. He was arrested and charged with the murders of Marcia Chapman, Cynthia Hinds, Opal Mills and Carol Ann Christensen, four of the women whose bodies had been found with his DNA.

On 5 November 2003, Gary Ridgway pleaded guilty to the aggravated first-degree murder of 48 women. His plea was part of a bargain to spare him the death penalty. He also agreed to cooperate in locating the remains of his victims.

Ridgway claimed that all of his victims had been killed in and around the Seattle area, though he disposed of some of them elsewhere in an attempt to confuse police. He also admitted to occasionally contaminating the dump sites with gum, cigarettes and written materials that belonged to others, to throw investigators off the scent. He confessed to killing 44 women between 1982 and 1984, but claimed to have killed only four thereafter – in 1986, 1987, 1990 and 1998.

Ridgway was given 48 life sentences. Since sentencing, he has confessed to yet more murders – a total of 71, although some speculate the true figure is closer to 150. It was a price, he claimed, worth paying for the betterment of society:

'I killed so many women I have a hard time keeping them straight.
I wanted to kill as many women that I thought were prostitutes as I possibly could.'

CHARLES SCHMID

IN NOVEMBER 1965, a 19-year-old from Tucson, Arizona, called Richard Bruns flew to stay with his grandmother in Columbus, Ohio, and went to the local police. He said he had information about murders that had taken place in Tucson, and was worried for his girlfriend whom he'd had to leave behind there and who knew the murderer well. The name of the killer whom he wanted arrested was Charles Schmid.

Schmid, known as Smitty, was a rich kid of 23, whose parents owned a nursing-home and had given him a cottage of his own at the bottom of their garden. He was also short – and bothered by it. At high-school, he'd been a gymnast – he'd even won a state championship. But now he wore high-heeled boots, which he stuffed with paper to make himself look even taller. The fact that this made him walk somewhat bizarrely he explained by saying he'd been crippled by Mafia hoods. This was fairly typical of Smitty, who felt inadequate with people of his own age, but who attracted local teenagers with his fantasies. He even got them to join his so-called sex club.

The first girl to disappear, on 31 May 1964, was 15-year-old Alleen Rowe, whose mother found her 'out on a date' when she got back late at night. She never returned, and her mother was later to remember a conversation she'd had with her daughter. Alleen had talked about being invited to join a sex club. 'You've got to be in, or you're a nobody,' she'd said.

Then, 15 months later, the two daughters of a Tucson doctor, Gretchen and Wendy Fritz, 17 and 13 respectively, also disappeared – followed a few weeks later by a 15-year-old called Sandra Hughes, who failed one day to return from school. Though the police did what they could, and talked to everyone who knew them, they failed to turn up any evidence.

The fact is that the fascinated teenagers who'd gathered around Schmid weren't talking, either to their parents or to the police, though it was more or less common knowledge among them that he'd killed at least Alleen Rowe. With a girlfriend he'd put to work in his parents' nursing home and a teenager called John Saunders, he'd inveigled Alleen out of her mother's house and had driven her off into the desert, where the two men had raped her, beaten her head in with rocks and buried her in a shallow grave. As for the doctor's daughters, the elder one, Gretchen, had been Smitty's girlfriend, but had become too possessive, so he'd strangled them both at the cottage and had then dumped their bodies outside town.

The reason that Richard Bruns knew this was because Schmid had boasted to him about it and he had called what he thought was Schmid's bluff. 'Show me!' So Schmid had driven him to where he'd left the bodies, and had then forced Bruns to help him bury them.

Even before Bruns's testimony, though, the police had begun to believe that Schmid had to be involved. For in a bizarre episode he'd been arrested on the beach at San Diego, California, interviewing girls in bikinis while posing as an FBI officer.

The story he'd given was equally odd: he said he'd been helping a couple of 'Mafia heavies' – who'd been hired by the Fritz family – in their investigations into the disappearance of Gretchen and Wendy.

Bruns, now back in Tucson, led the police out to what remained of the two girls; Smitty, John Saunders and the girlfriend, Mary French, were all arrested. As the case unfolded in court, parents were horrified at what their sons and daughters had got up to. There was talk of teenage prostitution-rings and orgies fuelled by drugs and booze, and Smitty later boasted about teaching a string of teenage paramours 'a hundred different ways to make love.'

Tried for the murder of Alleen Rowe, Mary French, who'd stayed in the car while Alleen was raped and killed, was sentenced to four-to-five years in prison; John Saunders, to life; and Charles Schmid, to death – commuted later to life after the banning of capital punishment. For the killing of the Fritz sisters, he received an extra 55 years.

His days of fantasizing, though, were not yet quite over. For in November 1972, he escaped from Arizona State Prison, along with another three-time killer, Raymond Hudgens. The two men held four people hostage on a ranch near Tempe, and then decided to separate. They were both picked up a few days later.

'DUTCH' SCHULTZ

'DUTCH' SCHULTZ WASN'T Dutch at all – he was German, and his last name wasn't Schultz – it was Flegenheimer. His father kept a saloon and livery-stable in what was known as Jewish Harlem, but deserted his family in 1916, and that was enough for son Arthur. After coming out of jail at the age of 16, from an 18-month stretch for burglary, he borrowed the name of a legendary member of the old Frog Hollow Gang, and got down to business.

A chorus girl once said that he looked like Bing Crosby with his face bashed in. Dutch certainly was no beauty – but then he didn't have to be. For by the mid '20s, after riding shotgun on Arnold Rothstein's liquor-trucks, he'd put together the toughest gang in New York. They ran protection for some of the toniest uptown restaurants. They were into slot machines and the numbers racket; liquor, restaurants, labour unions, gambling, and fixing any horse-race or boxing-match they could. By the beginning of the '30s, Dutch – who had a reputation for miserliness – was said to be making $20 million a year.

He didn't get to the top by any subtlety. He simply beat up or got rid of anyone who stood in his way. He out-muscled his competition – he arrived in the numbers racket, for example, by simply calling a meeting, laying his .45 on the table and saying, 'I'm your partner.' When 'Legs' Diamond had to get out of New York after killing a drunk, Dutch took over his liquor trucks; and then, when Legs objected, had him killed.

He avoided arrest in the usual way, by paying off the police and providing campaign funds and votes to all the politicians who mattered – particularly district attorney William Copeland Dodge. But a noose of prosecutions gradually settled round his neck. He beat the rap on a tax-evasion charge in Syracuse in 1933, but in 1935 he faced another, this time put together by special prosecutor Thomas Dewey. His lawyers eventually succeeded in having the trial moved to a little upstate town, but the consensus was, in 'Lucky' Luciano's words, that 'the loudmouth is never coming back.'

Dutch, though, spent months in tiny Malone, New York, before the trial, schmoozing the inhabitants, dressing modestly and even converting to Catholicism in the town's little church. When he got off, he told reporters: 'This tough world ain't no place for dunces. And you can tell all those smart guys in New York that the Dutchman is no dunce.'

The 'smart guys in New York,' though, didn't want the Dutchman on their turf any more. Mayor Fiorello La Guardia sent a message warning him not to come back, and started literally breaking up his gambling empire – he had himself photographed on barges taking a sledgehammer to Dutch's slot-machines. Thomas Dewey started preparing another case, this time against his restaurant rackets and his operation began to leak at the seams as other mobsters moved in on it.

He was exiled to Newark, New Jersey, where he set up his headquarters in a restaurant called the Palace Chop House. Then, sometime in late autumn 1935 – after having to kill one of his own lieutenants for conspiring with Luciano – he called a meeting of the Syndicate and demanded the assassination of Thomas Dewey. The Syndicate refused: it was far too high-profile. He said, fine, he'd kill Dewey himself – and so signed his own death warrant. In October, with his lieutenants, he was gunned down in the Palace Chop House by assassins from Murder Incorporated. He was 33.

'BUGSY' SIEGEL

BENJAMIN 'BUGSY' SIEGEL was there right at the beginning of the new-look New York Mafia. He was in the jail-cell where 'Lucky' Luciano first got together with Meyer Lansky. He was one of the four gunmen who murdered Giuseppe Masseria; and one of the four 'internal-revenue agents' who were in at the kill of Salvatore Maranzano, the ruthless would-be *Capo di Tutti Capi* of the city's underworld. He was also appointed to the board of the Unione Siciliana, one of the first attempts at a commission to guide the power of the Mafia nationwide. He may not have understood much about the politics – he started out as a small-time car-thief and driver of booze-trucks, after all – and he left that sort of thing, in any case, to Luciano and Lansky. But he knew all the right people; he was presentable; and, in 1935, he must have seemed the ideal choice to spearhead the New York families' expansion of operations to the West Coast.

Teaming up in southern California with a local mob led by Jack Dragna, Siegel ran drugs and operated a string of gambling-clubs and offshore casino-ships on behalf of his New York bosses both before and during the War. With the help of his pal, actor George Raft – and with his rough edges smoothed off by a divorced millionairess called Countess Dorothy Di Frasso – he was at ease in the best Hollywood circles. He was on first-name terms with people like Jean Harlow, Clark Gable and Gary Cooper – and a magnet to every starlet. He fitted right in. As he said,

'Class, that's the thing that counts in life. Without class and style, a man's a bum; he might just as well be dead.'

Gambling and stars: it was this combination that was to lead to Siegel's one major contribution to Mafia history. For in 1945, he suggested to his bosses the idea of building a casino and hotel in the Nevada desert at a place called Las Vegas. He put up $3 million, and the Commission soon organized a loan to match his investment. The place, he said, would be called The Flamingo – a name suggested by his girlfriend Virginia Hill – and there'd be a grand opening, with all of Hollywood's royalty there.

Word soon got back to the centre, though, that money was disappearing during The Flamingo's building, some of it salted away abroad, and a decision was taken at an informal meeting of bosses in Havana, Cuba, that Siegel would have to repay with interest the East Coast Mafia investment as soon as the hotel-casino opened. Trouble was, the grand opening that Siegel had planned turned out a disaster. Bad weather kept planes grounded at LA airport; the stars never showed. In two weeks, The Flamingo was closed after losing $100,000.

'Bugsy' couldn't pay, and his old friends in New York could no longer protect him. It was a matter of business; an example had to be set. So on the night of 20 June 1947, Siegel was gunned down as he sat in the living-room of Virginia Hill's Los Angeles house on North Linden Drive. The final bullet, the 'calling card,' was fired into his left eye. Just five people went to his funeral.

RICHARD SPECK

IN A NURSES' hostel in Chicago in the early hours of 14 July 1966, Richard Speck was responsible for what was later called 'the most bestial rampage in the city's history.' If he hadn't been so bad at counting and so expert at tying knots, the good-looking 24-year-old sailor might never have been caught.

Just before midnight on 13 July, a 23-year-old nurse called Corazon Amurao opened her door to find a strange man wearing a dark jacket and trousers and smelling of alcohol pointing a gun at her. He forced her at gunpoint into another room where three other nurses were sleeping. Soon nine nurses were gathered together and herded into a bedroom, where the unknown man cut bed sheets into strips with a knife as they lay on the floor, and then bound and gagged them. He said that he wouldn't harm them, he only wanted money, but when that had all been collected, he sat on the bed looking at them, fingering his knife.

Then, one by one, he took seven of them out of the room to various parts of the building and knifed or strangled them to death. For the last one – or so he thought – he reserved special treatment: he raped and sodomized her where she lay for 25 minutes before killing her.

He'd forgotten, however, about Corazon Amurao, who'd hidden herself during one of his absences under a bunk bed. After he'd left and when she thought it finally safe to move, she managed to get outside to a balcony and scream for help.

When the police arrived, they found mutilated corpses, mayhem, bedrooms awash with blood. But they also had a witness who could give them a description. The killer, she said, was pock-marked; had a tattoo on his arm with the words 'Born to raise hell'; and had talked about needing money to get to New Orleans. This – together with the square knots he'd used to tie up his victims – immediately suggested to the police that he might be a seaman. And half a block away was the hiring hall of the National Maritime Union.

They soon discovered that a man answering to Ms. Amurao's description had visited the hiring hall enquiring about a ship to New Orleans, and had filled out an application form in the name of Richard E. Speck. There was a photograph and a contact number, which turned out to belong to Speck's sister. With a positive ID from Corazon Amurao in hand, they called Speck's sister with the offer of a job. But though Speck himself called back within half an hour, he never turned up for the 'interview'. So detectives started scouring sailors' haunts – hotels, flophouses and bars – across the city.

They quickly came across Speck's tracks: a hotel where he'd picked up two prostitutes on the night after the murders; another he'd checked out from half an hour before they came. He was finally arrested only after they'd named him as their chief suspect and released his description and photograph to the media. For a surgeon at Cook County Hospital, examining an emergency patient who'd been admitted after slashing his wrists, remembered a tattoo he'd read about in his newspaper that day.

Richard Speck was tried and sentenced – first to death, then after commutation to several centuries in prison – for first-degree murder. The seaman – who'd regularly worked the ore-barges in the Great Lakes – had a record of violence towards women and may have killed several times before the attack on the hostel. For there had been a rash of unsolved murders in

Benton Harbor, Michigan, earlier that year when Speck was in the area, and another in Monmouth, Illinois, where he'd gone on to stay with his brother. On 2 July 1966, five days after he'd been let go from an ore-boat in Indiana Harbor, three girls who'd been swimming not far away had disappeared.

BRENDA SPENCER

TEENAGED BRENDA, THROUGH no particular fault of her own, was trouble. Her mother was long gone, and she lived with her father who not only couldn't get her in line, but was also feckless and irresponsible. She played hookey from school; she stole; she messed around with drugs. But she also loved guns. She liked to shoot birds and once used her BB gun to shoot out the windows of the elementary school opposite their house. So what does Brenda's father do for his little girl? For Christmas 1978, he buys her a semi-automatic .22 calibre rifle and about 500 rounds of ammunition.

Within a matter of days, Brenda started digging a tunnel in the family's backyard as a hiding-place. She also moved her collection of weapons to the garage. Then on the morning of 29 January, she struck. When the principal of the elementary school opposite arrived to open the gate for waiting children, she shot both him and the janitor. She wounded nine children and a policeman who tried to help out in a 20-minute barrage.

Over the next several hours, hiding in the besieged house, she explained herself on the telephone to police and reporters. She said:

'I just started shooting. That's it. I just did it for the fun of it. I just don't like Mondays. . . I did this because it's a way to cheer up the day. Nobody likes Mondays.'

After a six-hour standoff, she gave herself up; and America started one of its periods of soul-searching about guns and the ubiquity of violence on television – to which Brenda had been addicted. Then, after she was convicted of murder and assault – and given two concurrent sentences of 48 years and 25-years-to-life – she was more or less forgotten. She did, though, leave one small enduring monument: Bob Geldof and the

Boomtown Rats' deadpan rock masterpiece based on her shooting spree, *I Don't Like Mondays*.

CHARLES STARKWEATHER AND CARIL ANN FUGATE

CHARLES STARKWEATHER, AGED 19, wore thick spectacles. He was bow-legged, red-haired, just 5 foot 2 inches tall – and a garbageman in Lincoln, Nebraska. He was also extremely sensitive. And when the parents of his 14-year-old girlfriend, Caril Ann Fugate, said something he didn't like as he waited for her one day at their house, he simply shot them with his hunting-rifle. Caril Ann, when she got back, didn't seem to mind one way or the other, so he went upstairs and killed her two-year-old half-sister to stop her crying, before settling down with Caril Ann to eat sandwiches in front of the television.

It was 19 January 1958, and, having put up a sign on the front door saying 'Every Body is Sick with the Flu,' the couple lived in the house for two days. Then, just before the bodies were discovered, they took off in Starkweather's hot rod, driving across America like his hero James Dean – and left a string of murders in their wake.

First to die was a wealthy 70-year-old farmer, whose car they stole when theirs got stuck in the mud. A few hours later, another farmer found the body of a teenage couple in a storm cellar – the girl had been repeatedly raped before being beaten to death. Soon afterwards, there were three more corpses to add to the tally. A rich Nebraskan businessman had been stabbed and shot inside his doorway. Upstairs his wife and their housekeeper had been tied up before being stabbed and mutilated.

There was one more death to come, that of a car-driving shoe-salesman in Douglas, Wyoming. But as the pair tried to make a getaway, one of the cars refused to start. A passer-by stopped and was ordered at gun-point to help release the hand-brake. Instead he grappled with Starkweather, who wrenched himself free and drove off at speed, leaving Caril Ann behind him. A police car – part of the force of 1,200 policemen and National Guardsmen who were by now searching for two killers – soon spotted him and gave chase. Starkweather's windshield was shattered by gunfire and he gave himself up. The man known as 'Little Red' then made a confession,

Charles and Caril Ann – the inspiration for Terrence Malick's Badlands.

proclaiming his hatred of a society full of 'Goddam sons of bitches looking for somebody to make fun of,' before dying in the electric chair in Nebraska State Penitentiary on 25 June 1959.

Caril Ann claimed that she'd been kidnapped and was innocent, but she wasn't believed. She was sentenced to life and let out of prison, on parole, 28 years later.

The murderous couple were to inspire many artists, including Terrence Malick, the reclusive director, who made his debut film, *Badlands*, about the couple, and Bruce Springsteen, whose haunting song *Nebraska* is based on their killing spree.

ROBERT STROUD

AS A PRISONER, Robert Stroud was unusually fortunate: at Leavenworth he had a double-size cell all to himself. But then he was a legend, perhaps the most famous prisoner in the entire United States penal system, the man who was to become known as The Birdman of Alcatraz.

Stroud was also, though, a murderer. In 1906, at the age of 19, he'd killed an Alaskan barman who'd refused to pay $10 for one of his whores. For this he was sentenced to 12 years in federal prison, first on Macneil Island in the pacific Northwest, and then at the Leavenworth Penitentiary in Kansas. He was a solitary man who seems to have cared nothing at all for other prisoners – only for the canaries he was allowed to keep, about which he already had a vast knowledge; one can only imagine that it was some slur on, or threat to, them that caused him to kill again. For in March 1916, not long before he was to be released, he knifed to death a guard in the Leavenworth mess hall. He later said laconically to a fellow convict:

'The guard took sick and died all of a sudden. He died of heart trouble. I guess you would call it a puncture of the heart... I never have given any reason for doing it, so they won't have much to work on; only that I killed him, and... I admit that much.'

This time Stroud was sentenced to hang. But his mother petitioned President Wilson, citing his work on canaries and their diseases, about which he already knew as much as anyone in the country. Eight days before he was due to go to the gallows, the President's wife Elizabeth Wilson – who had taken over most of the President's duties after he'd had a heart attack – granted a reprieve. Stroud's sentence was commuted to life in solitary confinement.

And that's how he spent the rest of it: in solitary, except for his birds. In 1943, he published a book, *Digest of Bird Diseases*, and he was later transferred to Alcatraz, where his work went on. He died of natural causes in Springfield, Missouri, in 1963, at the age of 76.

DR JOHN WHITE WEBSTER

DR JOHN WHITE Webster is perhaps the only Harvard professor ever to have been hanged in public, though there are many – particularly students – who might have wished others despatched the same way. He murdered a close friend of his, a rich benefactor of the Massachusetts Medical College, where White also lectured; and the eminence of the two people involved – and the reason for the murder – excited, in the language of the times, 'much comment.'

The reason for the murder was debt. For Webster had often borrowed money from his victim, the eccentric Dr George Parkman, known – because of his jutting jaw – as 'Chin'. He'd pledged as security for the loans his well-known collection of minerals. But he'd also pledged it to another creditor, and when 'Chin' Parkman heard about this, he was furious. On the morning of 23 November 1849, he went off to see Webster at his laboratory for a showdown.

He never returned. The river was dragged, but no trace of him was found – until, that is, the caretaker, who hated Webster, broke his way into his laboratory three days later and discovered in the light of his torch what looked like the remains of a human pelvis.

Webster'd done his best to cover his tracks. On the day of Parkman's disappearance, he'd told the agent who collected his lecture fees that he'd paid Parkman all the money he owed him, and two days later he'd repeated the same story to the Parkman family, suggesting that he might have been killed after he left the laboratory for the cash he was by then carrying.

Unfortunately for him, though, the caretaker had by that time started wondering why Webster was up all night working in the laboratory, with his medical furnace constantly burning – and why he double-locked the lab doors whenever he went out.

The ashes in Webster's medical furnace were subsequently raked out, and found to contain, not only the remains of human bones, but also a set of false teeth. Webster claimed they belonged to a corpse he'd been dissecting. He repeated the story that he'd paid off Parkman's debt and he produced witnesses who swore that they'd seen Parkman alive well after the time of his supposed murder. It was the shape of Parkman's jaw, however – and the evidence of the dentist who'd had to fit teeth to it – which finally did him in. He was found guilty of murder after a nine-day hearing.

The professor was not quite done yet. Though he now confessed to the murder, he said that Parkman had been so insulting he'd lashed out at him in rage: he hadn't intended to kill him; and he asked for the charge against him to be reduced to manslaughter. The Council of Massachusetts refused and the professor was hanged, in front of 150 people, on 30 August 1850.

PHILLIP GARRIDO

PHILLIP CRAIG GARRIDO was born on 5 April 1951 in Contra Costa County, California. His father Manuel, a forklift operator, provided a modest, yet comfortable home. Phillip's anti-social behaviour began with a motorcycle accident as a teenager. Before the tragic event, claimed his dad, Phillip had been a 'good boy'. Afterwards, he became uncontrollable and started to take illegal drugs.

The year was 1969, a time when American counterculture was pervasive. Phillip grew his hair, bought a fringed leather jacket and played bass in a psychedelic rock group. But in reality, the young high school graduate wanted little to do with peace and love. Eighteen years old, Phillip had already committed his first act of rape, and would regularly beat his girlfriend, Christine Perreira.

In 1972, he was charged with the rape of a 14-year-old girl whom he had plied with barbiturates. Phillip avoided doing time in prison when the girl refused to testify. Once clear of the rape charge, Phillip married Christine. The young couple settled 300 km (185 miles) northeast in South Lake Tahoe.

Christine got a job dealing cards at Harrah's Casino, while her husband pursued his dream of becoming a rock star. Three years passed, and each day was blanketed in a haze induced by marijuana, cocaine and LSD. Phillip would spend hours masturbating while watching elementary school girls across the street, but the real object of his interest was a woman. Phillip had been following her for months, during which he developed a very elaborate plan, which he set in motion by renting a warehouse in

Reno, 100 km (60 miles) to the south. He then fixed up the space, hanging rugs for soundproofing. A mattress was brought in, as were satin sheets, bottles of wine and pornographic magazines.

When his trap was set, Phillip took four tabs of LSD and attacked the woman. However, due to his drugged state, she managed to fight him off. Frustrated, Phillip drove to Harrah's, where he asked one of his wife's co-workers, Katie Callaway Hall, for a ride home. Katie was not as lucky as the intended victim. She ended up being raped repeatedly in the warehouse. After eight hours of pain and humiliation, Katie was rescued by a police officer whose eye had been drawn to the door, which had been left ajar.

This time, Christine did not stand by Phillip. After her husband's arrest, she severed all ties. The divorce came through just as Phillip was beginning a 50-year prison sentence in Leavenworth, Kansas.

However, for Phillip, romance was still in the air. He began corresponding with the niece of a fellow inmate, Nancy Bocanegra, four years his junior. In 1981, the two were married in a ceremony conducted by the prison chaplain. Religion, it seemed, had turned into the focus of his life. A Catholic by birth, he converted, becoming a Jehovah's Witness. Phillip's extreme devotion to the denomination was cited by the prison psychologist as an indication that he would commit no further crimes.

Phillip was granted parole in 1988. With Nancy in tow, he returned to South Lake Tahoe, where they spent nearly three uneventful years.

On 10 June 1991, Phillip's prison psychologist would be proven wrong. That morning, a man named Carl Probyn watched in horror as his 11-year-old stepdaughter was dragged into a grey sedan. Several of the girl's friends had also witnessed the abduction – and yet no one was able to provide the licence plate number of the car that sped away.

The girl, Jaycee Dugard, soon found herself living in sheds, tents and under tarpaulins in the backyard of a house on Walnut Avenue, Antioch, Contra Costa County. The property belonged to Phillip's mother, who suffered from dementia. Eventually, the old woman would be shipped off to a chronic care hospital. Jaycee, of course, remained on the property, where she would be subjected to 18 years of sexual abuse at Phillip's hands. She bore her captor two children, both daughters, born in 1994 and 1997. Both would come to describe Jaycee as an older sister.

Phillip ran a print shop, Printing for Less, but he had very few repeat customers. That's because those who gave him business were often subjected to bizarre ramblings. Some customers were shown a machine, through which the printer claimed he could communicate with God. Others might be treated to songs that Phillip had written about his attraction to underage girls.

In August of 2009, he walked into the San Francisco offices of the FBI to hand-deliver two weighty tomes he had written: *The Origin of Schizophrenia Revealed* and *Stepping into the Light*. The latter was a personal story in which Phillip detailed how it was that he had come to triumph over his violent sexual urges. He approached Lisa Campbell, a special events coordinator at the University of California, Berkeley, with the idea of a lecture. Phillip was not alone when he made his proposal. Both his daughters sat in on the meeting, listening intently as their father spoke about his deviant past and the rapes he had committed.

It was Campbell's report of this strange behaviour to Phillip's parole officer that eventually brought an end to Jaycee's nightmare. When confronted, on 26 August 2009, Phillip admitted to kidnapping Jaycee, adding that he was the father of her children. Both he and Nancy were taken into custody.

On 28 April 2011, Phillip pleaded guilty to Jaycee's kidnapping, as well as 13 counts of sexual assault. Sitting next to her husband, Nancy pleaded guilty to the kidnapping, and one charge of aiding and abetting a sexual assault.

Nancy's sentence was not nearly as harsh as that of her husband. Where Phillip received a term amounting to 431 years, Nancy was sentenced to 36 years in prison. Should she live a long life, Nancy Garrido will be 90 when she leaves prison.

WAYNE WILLIAMS

IN THE EARLY hours of 22 May 1981, police on watch near a bridge over the Chattahoochee River in Atlanta, Georgia, heard a sudden splash, and later saw a young black man driving away from the scene in a station-wagon. When they stopped the car, the driver identified himself as 23-year-old Wayne Williams, a music-promoter and freelance photographer, and he was allowed to go. The police, though, remained suspicious and put Williams under surveillance; when a body was discovered in the river two days later, they pulled him in.

The body was that of a 27-year-old black man, whom a witness later said he'd seen together with Williams, holding hands coming out of a cinema. Dog-hairs found on the corpse were found to match samples of those found in Williams' house and in his car. It was, it seemed, an open-and-shut case. But a question remained: was Wayne Williams a serial killer? Was it he who'd been responsible for the deaths of 26 young blacks, teenagers and children in Atlanta over the past two years?

The first disappearances and discoveries had caused little fuss, given the city's high crime rate. Two teenagers had been found dead by a lake in July 1979; another had disappeared two months later. The fourth case, it was true, had caused some to-do, since the missing nine-year-old boy was the son of a locally well-known ex-civil rights worker. But it wasn't until the number of disappearances had mounted and the bodies had begun to pile up that the police started to take serious notice.

By the time a year was over, seven young blacks had been murdered – one of them a 12-year-old girl tied to a tree and raped – and three more were still missing. The police were by now being accused of protecting a white racist killer. A number of bereaved parents formed a group and held a press conference to say that, even if the killer was black, the police were still not doing enough, simply because none of the victims was white. The police argued back that a white person, picking up kids in black neighbourhoods, would have stood out a mile and that the killer was probably a black teenager, someone who could get his victims' trust.

None of this, though, made any difference, for the killings went on. Within a month, two more black children had disappeared; and the body count kept rising. One boy went missing that September; another in the following month. Civic groups offered a reward of $100,000; special programmes were offered to keep black kids off the streets; a curfew was even imposed. But the disappearances and the number of bodies discovered continued to rise. By May 1981, there were 26 dead, with one black kid still missing. The police had no leads at all. They were only watching the river that night because that's where the latest victim had been found.

With Wayne Williams in custody, though, they did at least have a suspect; and, quite suddenly, they had witnesses who said they'd seen Williams with both the men found in the river. Others came forward to say that he'd tried to have sex with them, and one of these linked him to yet another victim The police then re-examined a number of the dead and found on eight others not only dog-hairs, but also fabric and carpet fibres that matched those in Williams's bedroom.

Williams was only tried for the murders of the two men found in the river. The evidence against him was entirely circumstantial, but it was reinforced when the judge reluctantly allowed evidence from the other murders to be admitted. Gradually a picture of Williams was formed: the son of two schoolteachers who had grown up gifted and indulged, he had turned into a man obsessed with the idea of success – he worked on the fringes of showbusiness. He also seemed to hate black people, even though he handed out leaflets offering black youths between the ages of 11 and 21 help with their musical careers.

Wayne Williams was found guilty on both counts of murder and sentenced to two consecutive life terms. Though many believed he was a scapegoat – and had been railroaded by the police – the murders of young blacks in Atlanta stopped with his imprisonment.

AILEEN WUORNOS

EVERYTHING WAS AGAINST Aileen Wuornos, right from the beginning. Her father deserted her mother before she was born and her mother ran off from Rochester, Michigan, not long afterwards, leaving her and her elder brother in charge of her grandparents, both of whom were drunks. Her grandfather beat both his wife and them; he allowed no friends in the house and wouldn't even let them open the curtains. Malnourished and unable to concentrate in school, the children took to lighting fires with firelighter for amusement, and at the age of six, Aileen's face was badly burned, scarred for life. By the time she reached puberty, she was already putting out to boys for food and drink, uppers, anything she could get. At 13 she was raped by a friend of her grandparents. At 14, she was pregnant – and the child, she said, could have been anybody's: the rapist's, her grandfather's, even her brother's. The baby, a son, was put up for adoption immediately after birth.

Then, when her grandmother died of cancer in 1971, she and her brother were thrown out of their grandfather's house and became wards of court.

She dropped out of school and took up prostitution, while her brother robbed stores to feed an increasing drugs habit. Soon after her grandfather committed suicide in 1976, her brother died of throat cancer. He was only 21, a year older than she.

As if all this wasn't enough, even her own genes seemed to be against her. For, quite apart from the cancers, the drinking and the suicide, the father she never met turned out to be a paranoid schizophrenic and a convicted paedophile. After spending time in mental hospitals for sodomizing children as young as ten, he hanged himself in a prison cell.

She had a couple of chances to go straight, it's true. She was picked up while hitchhiking by an older man, who became besotted with her and married her, and she also got $10,000 from a life-insurance policy her brother had taken out. But the husband she abused and beat, and she used the insurance money to buy a fancy car, which she promptly crashed. So she was soon back on the road as a hitchhiking hooker, hanging out with bikers, and getting regularly arrested: for cheque forgery, breaches of the peace, car-theft, gun-theft and holding up a convenience store. For the latter, she did a year in jail, and when she came out, she tried to commit suicide.

Then, though, in 1986, Aileen, by now known as Lee, met 22-year-old Tyria 'Ty' Moore in a Daytona Beach gay bar and she turned out to be the love of her life – all the love that she'd never had. They rented an apartment together; they worked at motels and bars while Aileen turned tricks on the side. Her looks, though, weren't getting any better – and at some point Aileen decided that Ty shouldn't have to work any more: she, after all, was Ty's 'husband.' That's when she started to kill.

Beginning at the end of 1989, there was a string of deaths that soon had police baffled. All were men; some were found naked; and they'd all been killed by the same small-calibre gun. They included a trucker, a rodeo worker, a heavy-machine-operator, even a child-abuse investigator. A 60-year-old missionary had disappeared.

There was only one clue to the killer's identity. For shortly before the missionary's car was identified as having been involved in an accident, two women were seen hurt, walking away. The police released sketches to the press and Ty and Lee were identified by several people. By now, Lee had also pawned the possessions of many of her victims, and she'd left her finger- or thumb-prints – as per Florida law – on the pawn-shop receipts.

Once the police identified what she'd pawned as belonging to the victims, it was only a matter of time.

There was one final betrayal. Ty, to save herself, went to the Florida police, and then, via a taped call to Aileen after she'd been arrested, persuaded her to confess. She did, but she said that every one of her victims had beaten and raped her. She wasn't believed. In two trials, first for one of the murders, and then for another three, she was condemned to death,

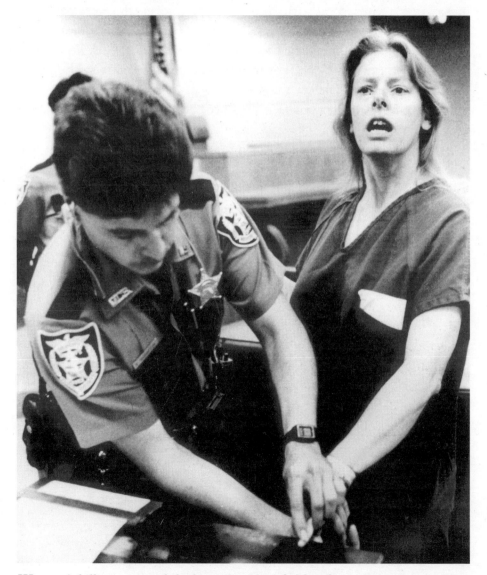

Wuornos's killing spree ended when police identified her fingerprints on stolen goods.

even though her defence had tried to present her as terminally damaged, with a borderline personality disorder.

Almost immediately, her story was told in a made-for-TV movie. Feminist writers defended her; an Aileen Wuornos Defense Group was set up. However, in 1999, she admitted that the claims she had made about beatings and rape had been entirely made up. But she also said that the police had delayed five months before arresting her, because they were negotiating a movie deal with Hollywood producers who were desperate for the real-life story of a female serial killer. There is perhaps some truth in this. In his 2003 documentary *The Selling of a Serial Killer*, Nick Broomfield claims that there was a meeting to discuss exclusive rights to the police investigation a month before she was arrested.

On Death Row, Wuornos seems to have had a religious conversion. She said:

'I believe I am totally saved and forgiven by Jesus Christ,'

and added that there were angels waiting for her on the other side. She was executed in late 2002.

UNITED KINGDOM

IAN BRADY AND MYRA HINDLEY

IAN BRADY AND Myra Hindley did everything they could to co-opt Hindley's 17-year-old brother-in-law David Smith. For he was promising raw material: he'd been in trouble with the law from the age of 11 and he liked to drink. So they fed him booze and the books of the Marquis de Sade. They took him out onto the moors for target-practice shooting and Brady continually dropped hints to him there: about murder, and the photography and burial of bodies.

Then, in October 1965, they decided finally to pull him in. The 23-year-old Hindley used a pretext to get Smith late at night to the house where she and Brady lived on a public-housing estate in Manchester; and then she pushed him into the living room as soon as she heard Brady starting to attack Edward Evans, a young man they'd picked up earlier in the evening, with an axe. Smith, confused by drink, was a terrified witness to his eventual murder. But Brady and Hindley wanted more. So they passed him the axe, and told him that, with his fingerprints now on it, he was far

Ian Brady and Myra Hindley – the Moors Murderers.

too involved to be able to retreat. He was forced to help in trussing up the body and cleaning the blood from the floor, furniture and walls.

By the time he left, Smith had been persuaded to bring round a pram the next day to move the body to Brady's car. But when he went home, he told his horrified wife what had happened and the next day, shaking with fear, and armed with a knife and a screwdriver, he went to a telephone box to call the police.

The young victim's body was still in the house; and first Brady, then Hindley were arrested. But then, little by little, as the police searched both the house and Brady's car, the full extent of their murderous exploits emerged. For in the house was a collection of books on Nazism, sadism and torture – as well as dozens of photographs of Brady and Hindley on the moors. Three sheets of paper discovered in the car seemed to contain instructions about how to bury a body, and in a notebook kept by Brady, amid a list of seemingly random and made-up names, there was one that stood out: that of John Kilbride. Kilbride was a schoolboy who'd disappeared two years before; the police became convinced that Brady and Hindley had killed the 12-year-old and buried him on the moors.

Worse, though, was to come. For, while the police were digging up the moors, looking for Kilbride's body, a careful search of the books in the house produced a hidden left-luggage ticket for two suitcases which – once retrieved – were found to contain ammunition, coshes, pornographic books, photographs and a number of tapes. One collection of photographs proved to be pornographic pictures of a gagged, naked child: of ten-year-old Leslie Ann Downey, who'd disappeared 13 months after Kilbride. One of the tapes contained, buried amongst Christmas music, a live 16-minute recording of her rape, torture and murder.

The bodies of both Kilbride and Leslie Ann Downey were found on the moors; and the tape was played, to the horror of all those present – indeed of the entire country – at the subsequent trial of Brady and Hindley. Both pleaded not guilty. They had given the police no co-operation at all. But there could be no doubt of their guilt, and the strong suspicion remains that they also killed two other children, Pauline Reade and Keith Bennett, who disappeared in 1963 and 1964 respectively.

For the murders of Edward Evans, John Kilbride and Leslie Ann Downey, Ian Brady was given three life sentences; Myra Hindley two, with an extra seven years for 'receiving, comforting and harbouring'. Later denied both appeal and release, she died in prison in late 2002. Brady – easily the more sinister figure of the two – died in 2017.

WILLIAM BURKE AND WILLIAM HARE

WILLIAM BURKE AND William Hare will always remain linked, like Laurel and Hardy or (for British readers) Marks and Spencer. Alone, living in Edinburgh in the late 1820s, they were nothing: just a labourer and the keeper of a disreputable boarding house. But together they were Burke and Hare, the most famous body-snatchers of them all – even though they ended up differently. For Hare, who turned King's Evidence and was a witness at Burke's trial, died later in London, after living under an assumed name; and Burke went the way of their joint victims. After he was hanged, his body was dissected at a public lecture by the Professor of Surgery at Edinburgh University, and his skeleton can still be seen today in the University's Anatomical Museum.

It was in 1827 that the pair first met, when Burke, who'd been working on the building of the Union Canal, moved to Edinburgh with a woman called Helen Dougal. As fellow Irishmen, Burke and Hare had much in common; and when one of Hare's lodgers, an old army veteran, died – and Hare had it in mind to sell his body to an anatomist – who better to help carry it off to the house of the celebrated anatomist Dr Robert Knox than his new friend William Burke?

Until the passing of the Anatomy Act in 1832, every dead person, by law, was required to have a Christian burial. So it was extremely difficult for practising anatomists and their students to get hold of the necessary raw material, except from so-called body-snatchers, who dug up newly-buried corpses from churchyards. Otherwise the bodies of executed criminals were the best they could get. Knox, then, was delighted to accept the body from Burke and Hare, with few questions asked, and he paid more than seven and a half pounds for it. He also said that he'd take any more they might be able to get their hands on, with over ten pounds to be paid for a really fresh specimen in good condition.

Burke and Hare, thrilled by their windfall, spotted a gap in the market and, like good capitalists, soon filled it. They began to lure travellers, usually to Hare's boarding house, and ply them with drink. Once befuddled, they simply smothered them. At least 15 people went the same way, at prices ranging from eight to 14 pounds, until a couple who'd been staying with Burke and Helen Dougal one day spotted the body of a woman hidden under a pile of straw. They went to the police with what they'd seen.

Burke, after turncoat Hare gave evidence against him, was hanged on 28 January 1829 – and the others disappeared, Hare to London and Helen Dougal, it's said, to Australia. Dr Knox's house on Surgeon's Square was invaded by a mob – two of the victims had been well-known on the city's streets – and his University lectures were constantly interrupted by heckling. In the end he left Edinburgh and, unable to get another university position, ended his days as an obscure general practitioner in east London.

JOHN CHRISTIE

IN 1949, JOHN Christie, then 51, and a resident of 10 Rillington Place in Notting Hill in London, gave evidence at the Old Bailey against his upstairs neighbour Timothy Evans, who was on trial for murdering his baby daughter. The judge congratulated Christie on the clarity of his testimony, and Evans, a semi-literate truck-driver, was duly hanged. It was taken for granted that he had also killed his wife Beryl Evans, whose body had been found in a wash-house at the property. In fact, he'd earlier said as much when giving himself up.

Four years later, though, in March 1953, a man named Beresford Brown, who had sub-let John Christie's flat from him a few days before, found by accident a kitchen-cupboard door that had been papered over. He opened it and saw the naked back of a partly-mummified woman. He called the police, who quickly found two other women, hidden behind the first, carefully stuffed into the cupboard upright. There was another body, which turned out to be that of Christie's wife, buried beneath the dining-room floor. Two more female skeletons were later found in the garden, as well as a human femur propping up a fence.

The four women in the house – three young prostitutes and Christie's wife – had all been killed well after Evans's execution. So a warrant was immediately put out for Christie's arrest; he was recognized and taken in a week later as he stood quietly on Putney Bridge. He was confused and exhausted. But he quickly confessed to the murder of all six women, and later to that of Beryl Evans, though not that of her baby daughter.

Little by little it emerged that Christie, who had been beaten as a child and then mocked by girls in his teens, was largely impotent with living women. So beginning in 1943, he started killing them, inviting them to the house when his wife was away, and then gassing and strangling them before having sex with their corpses. In December 1952 he finally disposed of his wife as an inconvenience; he was then free to kill when he chose. His last three victims died over a period of a few days.

Did Christie kill Beryl Evans? And if so, why did Timothy Evans say he himself had killed her when he gave himself up in Wales? The answer is that Beryl had been pregnant and Evans had told Christie that they wanted

Christie with his wife, who was later found buried under the floorboards.

an abortion. Christie had offered to do it himself while Evans was at work. Then he persuaded Evans that Beryl had died during the operation and that if he didn't make a run for it, he, Evans, would be held responsible. He offered to have the Evans' daughter adopted by friends.

Before he was tried, Evans, who was mentally subnormal, had withdrawn his confession and had told this version of events to police, but he hadn't been believed. And after Christie was hanged on 15 July 1953, a campaign began to have the young truck-driver posthumously pardoned. Finally, 13 years later, a full enquiry was set up, headed by a High Court judge, who announced that, though Evans had probably murdered his wife, he had probably not murdered his daughter, the case for which he'd actually been tried. He was given his pardon. But though 10 Rillington Place, along with the rest of the street, has long since been torn down, a strong sense of injustice lingers...

DR HAWLEY HARVEY CRIPPEN

DR HAWLEY HARVEY, later Peter, Crippen is one of the most famous – and most reviled – murderers of the 20th century. Yet he was a small, slight man, intelligent, dignified, eternally polite and anxious for the welfare of those around him. With his gold-rimmed spectacles, sandy whiskers and shy expression, he was, in fact, more mouse than monster. His problem was his wife.

Crippen was born in Coldwater, Michigan, in 1862, and studied for medical degrees in Cleveland, London and New York. Around 1890, his first wife died, leaving him a widower; three years later, when working in a practice in Brooklyn, he fell in love with one of his patients, a 17-year-old with ambitions to be an opera singer, called Cora Turner. She was overweight; her real name was Kunigunde Mackamotzki – she was the boisterous, loose daughter of a Russian-Polish immigrant. But none of this mattered to Crippen. He first paid for her singing lessons, and then he married her.

In 1900, by now consultant physician to a mail-order medicine company, Crippen was transferred to London to become manager of the firm's head office and Cora came to join him. On arrival in London, though, she decided to change her name once again – this time to Belle Elmore – and to try out her voice in the city's music halls. She soon became a success and acquired many friends and admirers. She bleached her hair; became a leading light in the Music Hall Ladies Guild; and entertained the first of what were to be many lovers.

Increasingly contemptuous of her husband, whom she regarded as an embarrassment, she forced him first to move to a grand house in north London that he could ill afford, and then to act as a general dogsbody to the 'lodgers' she soon moved in.

Crippen took such consolation as he could with a shy secretary at his company called Ethel Le Neve. But in 1909, he lost his job, and his wife threatened to leave him, taking their life savings with her. By the beginning of the following year, he'd had enough. On 19 January, he acquired five grains of a powerful narcotic called hyoscine from a chemist's in New Oxford Street; and the last time his wife was seen was 12 days later, at a dinner for two retired music-hall friends at the Crippens' home. Two days after that, as it turned out, Crippen began pawning her jewellery, and sent a letter to the Music Hall Ladies Guild, saying that she'd had to leave for America, where a relative was seriously ill. Later he announced that she'd gone to the wilds of California; that she had contracted pneumonia; and, in March – after Ethel had moved into his house – that she had died there.

Two actors, though, who'd been touring in California returned to England and, when told, said they'd heard nothing at all about Cora's death. Scotland Yard took an interest and Crippen was forced to concede that he'd made up the story: his wife had in fact left for America with one of her lovers. Though this seemed to satisfy the detectives, he then made his first big mistake: he panicked, settled his affairs overnight and left with Ethel the next day for Europe, after persuading her to start a new life with him in America. When the police called again, it was to find them gone. They began a thorough search of the house. What remained of his wife – rotting flesh, skin and hair – was found buried under the coal cellar.

Unaware of the furore of horror created by this discovery in the British press, Crippen – his moustache shaved off, under an assumed name, and accompanied by Ethel, disguised as his son – took a ship from Antwerp to Quebec in Canada. But they were soon recognized by the captain who, aware of a reward, used the new invention of the wireless telegraph to send a message to his employers. Each day from then on, in fact, he sent via the same medium daily reports on the doings of the couple which were published in the British newspapers.

Meanwhile, Chief Inspector Dew of Scotland Yard took a faster ship and arrested Dr Crippen and 'son' Ethel when they reached Canadian waters.

Huge, angry crowds greeted them when they arrived back a month later, under arrest, in England. The newspapers had done their job of transforming the pair of them into vicious killers. But Crippen always maintained that Ethel had had absolutely no knowledge of the murder, and when they were tried separately, she was acquitted. Crippen, though, was found guilty and was hanged in Pentonville Prison on 23 November 1910. Before he died, he described Ethel as

> 'my only comfort for the past three years. . . As I face eternity, I say that Ethel Le Neve has loved me as few women love men. . . Surely such love as hers for me will be rewarded.'

It is not known whether she was rewarded, or indeed what became of her, though one story recounts that she ran a tea-shop in Bournemouth, under an assumed name, for 45 years...

CLAUDE DUVAL

CLAUDE DUVAL'S EPITAPH called him 'the Second Norman Conqueror' and there's no doubt at all that he was a 17th-century star. His biography was written by a professor of anatomy at Oxford University; he was the prototype for Macheath in John Gay's hugely successful *The Beggar's Opera* and his exploits were even noted approvingly by the famous historian Lord Macaulay. When he was finally caught in 1670, it's said that large numbers of rich and fashionable women tried to intercede on his behalf. Perhaps taking offence, King Charles II said no. So the ladies had to make do instead with veiled visits to see his hanged body as it lay in state for several days in London's Covent Garden.

Duval – whose biographer says was a card-sharp and confidence-trickster as well as a highwayman – was born in Normandy in 1643, but gravitated to Paris, where he fell in with Royalist exiles waiting for the death of Oliver Cromwell and the restoration of the British monarchy. At the age of 17, then, he crossed the Channel to London as a footman to the Duke of Richmond. But he didn't stay in service long. For the days of Puritan austerity were finally over: with the King setting an example, the gentry were dressing up in finery again, and taking to the roads to visit each other or to travel to their estates. It was an opportunity too good to miss.

Duval, then, became a holdup-man – but a holdup-man with a difference. For he was well-dressed, courteous and good-looking and it wasn't long before women travellers were having daydreams about being waylaid by him. On one occasion, he's said to have played the flute and danced with one of his pretty victims – giving up £300, a vast sum, for the privilege. On another, he gravely handed back a solid-silver bottle to a woman traveller who was feeding her baby with it.

As his legend grew, so did his standing in the most-wanted list published in the *London Gazette* and the reward offered for his capture. A road was named after him in Hampstead, near the site of one of his robberies. He became a byword for daring and glamour. Then, though, in January 1670, he was finally caught – and all too prosaically. He was recognized in a London pub run by an ex-mistress of the Duke of Buckingham called The Hole in the Wall (the name, much later, of Butch Cassidy and the Sundance Kid's retreat) and he was too drunk to put up much resistance.

Tried on six charges, he was soon condemned to death. But so popular had he become that at his hanging there were riots. His body was taken down by the crowd and carried to a tavern in St. Giles-in-the-Fields, where it lay, open to all-comers, for several days. Finally, after a long torchlit procession, Claude Duval was buried under the central aisle of St. Paul's Church in Covent Garden. His epitaph began:

'Here lies Du Vall: Reader, if male thou art,
Look to thy purse; if female to thy heart.'

RUTH ELLIS

RUTH ELLIS, BORN in Rhyl, Wales, in 1927, has the distinction of being the last woman in Britain to be hanged. Twenty-eight years old when she went to the scaffold, she was as much victim as killer.

Men, from the beginning, were Ruth Ellis's problem – and she theirs. Raised in Manchester – a waitress and for a while a dance-band singer –

she'd fallen in love at the age of 17 with an American flyer, only for him to be killed in action in 1944. Soon after his death she bore him a son and six years later she married a dentist and had a baby daughter by him – only for him to divorce her shortly afterwards on the grounds of mental cruelty. Now with two small children to take care of, and with no qualifications except her looks, she did what she had to. She became a club-hostess and hooker. She migrated to London and there, in Carrolls Club in 1953, she met a man called David Blakely.

Blakely was a racing driver, a sophisticated, debonair man, but he soon became obsessed with Ruth. He offered to marry her, but she refused, and while she played him along, she also took up with one of his friends. For a year or so she managed to keep both men happy. But by 1954 Blakely had become almost insanely jealous. He started to beat her. He gave her a black eye; he broke her ankle; he also started seeing other women. But when Ruth finally threw him out as a result, he came back like a whipped dog, once more begging her to marry him. Again Ruth refused, but by now, it seemed, they were doomed to each other.

They set up house together in Egerton Gardens in Kensington. But by now Blakely had a taste for infidelity. At the beginning of April 1955, Ruth Ellis had a miscarriage; a few days later Blakely said he had to go and see a mechanic who was building him a new car. She followed him to an apartment in Hampstead, and when she heard a woman's laughter inside, she knocked on the door and demanded to see him. He refused, and when she began to shout, the police were called.

The next day she returned. This time she saw Blakely coming down the steps arm-in-arm with a pretty young girl. She made up her mind. On the evening of 10 April, Easter Sunday, when she found him coming out of a Hampstead pub called the Magdala, she took a gun out of her handbag and shot him six times. She later told the police:

'I am guilty,'

and added,

'I am rather confused.'

At her trial in June of the same year, she confessed:

'I intended to kill him.'

It took the jury just 14 minutes to find her guilty. She was sentenced to death, and a month later, despite widespread protests, she was hanged. Her son, the child of the American pilot, committed suicide in 1982, following years of depression. Her daughter, in a newspaper interview a year later, said she couldn't get out of her mind the image of the hangman,

> 'peering through the peephole into her cell, trying to work out how much rope he should use to make sure that frail little neck was broken.'

Ruth Ellis, the last woman to be hanged in Britain.

JOHN HAIGH

IN 1949, WHEN he came to trial, John Haigh was headlined in the British press as the Vampire Killer. But the only evidence that he ever drank his victims' blood was his own – part of a ploy to have himself declared insane. In fact, he killed for money.

In 1944, as the Second World War was drawing to an end, Haigh, 34, was an independent craftsman, working part-time in a London pinball arcade owned by a man called Donald McSwann. It was McSwann who was his first victim. On some pretext, Haigh lured him down to the basement-workshop in the house he rented, and there beat him to death with a hammer. Then he dissolved his body in a vat of sulphuric acid, and poured what remained, grisly bucket by bucket, into the sewage system.

Nobody seemed to pay any attention to McSwann's disappearance. Haigh, who took over the pinball arcade, told his parents that their son had gone to ground in Scotland to avoid the draft; he himself went to Scotland every week to post a letter to them purporting to be from him. This worked so well that in July 1945 he sent them a further letter, asking them to visit 'his' dear friend, John Haigh, at his home. They did. They went downstairs to inspect the basement workshop – and followed their son into the sewers.

Haigh, with the help of forged documents, made himself the McSwanns' heir, the master of five houses and a great deal of money. But he was a gambler and a bad investor and within three years he was once more broke. So he searched out a new inheritance. He invited a young doctor and his wife to look at a new workshop he'd set up in Crawley in Surrey. They agreed...

By the time a year had passed, though, the pattern had repeated itself. Once again unable to pay his bills at the London residential hotel he by now lived in, he badly needed a fresh victim – and this was when he made his first mistake. For he chose someone much too close to him: a fellow-resident of the hotel, a rich elderly widow called Olive Durand-Deacon. Mrs Durand-Deacon, who ate her meals at the table next to him, was under the impression that Haigh was an expert in patenting inventions and she had an idea, she said, for false plastic fingernails. He charmingly invited her to his Crawley 'factory' to go over the details.

It took several days for the acid-bath to do its work on Mrs Durand-Deacon, and in the meantime Haigh had to go to the police, with another

Haigh was dubbed the Vampire Killer by the British press.

resident, to declare her missing. The police, from the beginning, were suspicious of him and, looking into his record, they found that he'd been imprisoned three times for fraud. So they searched the Crawley 'factory' and though they didn't find Mrs Durand-Deacon, by now reduced to a pile of sludge outside in the yard, they did find a revolver and a receipt for her coat from a cleaner's in a nearby town. They later discovered her jewellery, which Haigh had sold to a shop a few miles away.

When arrested and charged, Haigh blithely confessed, believing that, in the absence of his victim's body, he could never be found guilty. But when a police search team painstakingly went through the sludge, they found part of a foot, what was left of a handbag and a well-preserved set of false teeth, which Mrs Durand-Deacon's dentist soon identified as hers.

In the end, Haigh pleaded insanity. But after a trial that lasted only two days, the jury took 15 minutes to decide that he was both sane and guilty. The judge sentenced him to death. Asked if he had anything to say, Haigh said: 'Nothing at all.' He was hanged at Wandsworth prison on 6 August 1949.

NEVILLE HEATH

IN 1946, IN POST-WAR LONDON, Neville Heath looked just like the man he claimed to be: a dashing ex-Royal-Air-Force officer, a war hero. He had fair hair and blue eyes, an air of romantic recklessness and, like a man who has successfully cheated death, he loved to party. To women hungry for men he must have seemed made to measure: an embodiment of the gallantry that had led to victory – and of the newly carefree spirit of the times.

This nightclub Lothario, though, was not at all what he looked like. For not only was he a gigolo with a criminal record, but he also had the distinction of having been court-martialled by three separate services: by the British Air Force in 1937, the British Army in 1941, and the South African Air Force in 1945. His offences – for being absent without leave, stealing a car, issuing worthless cheques, indiscipline and wearing medals to which he wasn't entitled and the like – all pointed in one direction: Neville Heath was a con man and poseur. He used women for money after he'd got them into his bed – as he could all too easily. But he preferred – when that palled – to beat them.

In March 1945, after guests at a London hotel reported hearing screams, a house detective burst into a bedroom to find Heath brutally whipping a girl, naked and bound hand and foot, beneath him. Neither the hotel nor the girl wanted publicity, and within two months Heath was at it again – though this time with a more willing participant, a 32-year-old occasional film extra called Margery Gardner, known in London clubs as Ocelot Margie. In May, security in another hotel intervened late at night as she lay under Heath's lash.

Ocelot Margie, though, had no complaints to make. For she was a masochist, haunting the clubs in search of bondage and domination by any man she could find willing. She obviously found Heath to her taste. For a month later she arranged to meet him at a club, and then returned with him to the same hotel for a further session. She wasn't to make it out alive.

In the early afternoon of the following day, a chambermaid found her naked dead body. She had been tied at the ankles and murderously whipped, and she had extensive bruising on her face and chin, as if someone had used extreme violence to keep her mouth shut. Her nipples had been almost bitten off, and something unnaturally large had been shoved into her vagina and then rotated, causing extensive bleeding.

The police quickly issued Heath's name and description to the press. But by this time he was in the south-coast resort town of Worthing, meeting the parents of a young woman he had earlier seduced after a promise of marriage. He quickly told her – and later her parents – his version of the murder: that he had lent his hotel room to Gardner to use for a tryst with another man and had later found her dead. He sent a letter to the police in London to the same effect, adding that he would later send on to them the murder weapon he'd found on the scene. Then he disappeared.

The murder weapon, of course, never arrived. But the police still failed to issue a photograph of Heath, and so he was free on the south coast for another 13 days, posing, rather unimaginatively, as Group Captain Rupert Brooke – the name of a famously handsome poet who died in the First World War. During that time, a young woman holidaymaker vanished after having been seen having dinner with 'Brooke' at his hotel; and it was suggested that the 'Group Captain' should contact the police with his evidence. He finally did so, but was recognized and held for questioning. In the pocket of a jacket at his hotel police later found a left-luggage ticket for a suitcase, which contained, among other things, clothes labelled with the name 'Heath,' a woman's scarf and a blood-stained riding-crop.

On the evening of the day Heath was returned to London and charged, the naked body of his second victim was found in a wooded valley not far from his hotel. Her cut hands had been tied together; her throat had been slashed; and after death her body had been mutilated with a knife before being hidden in bushes. Heath, though, was never tried for this murder. He came to the Old Bailey on 24 September 1946 charged only with the murder of Margery Gardner – and he was quickly found guilty by the jury. He was hanged at London's Pentonville Prison the following month.

JACK THE RIPPER

NOW THAT LONDON'S famous fogs have disappeared – and with them the gas-lamps, the brick shacks, the crammed slums, the narrow streets and blind alleyways of the city's East End – it's hard to imagine the hysteria and terror that swept through the area when The Whitechapel Murderer – later known as Jack the Ripper – went to work. Already in 1888 two prostitutes had been murdered. So when the body of another was found, her throat cut and her stomach horribly mutilated, on 31 August, she was immediately assumed to be the brutal killer's third victim. And brutal he was:

'Only a madman could have done this,'

said a detective; the police surgeon agreed.

'I have never seen so horrible a case,'

he announced.

'She was ripped about in a manner that only a person skilled in the use of a knife could have achieved.'

A week later, the body of 'Dark Annie' Chapman was found not far away, this time disembowelled and with its uterus removed; and a fortnight after that, a letter was received by the Central News Agency in London which finally gave the killer a name. It read (in part):

'Grand job, that last job was. I gave the lady no time to squeal. I love my work and want to start again. You will soon hear from me, with my funny little game... Next time I shall clip the ears off and send them to the police just for jolly.'

It was signed:

'Jack the Ripper.'

Five days later, he struck again – twice. The first victim was 'Long Liz' Stride, whose body, its throat cut, was discovered on the night of 30 September by the secretary of a Jewish Working Men's Club whose arrival in a pony trap seems to have disturbed the Ripper. For apart from a nick on one ear, the still-warm corpse was unmutilated. Unsatisfied, the Ripper went on to find another to kill. Just 45 minutes later – and 15 minutes' walk away – the body of Catherine Eddowes, a prostitute in her 40s, was found. Hers was the most mutilated so far. For her entrails had been pulled out through a large gash running from her breastbone to her abdomen; part of one of her kidneys had been removed and her ears had been cut off. A trail of blood led to a ripped fragment of her apron, above which had been written in chalk:

'The Juwes are The men That Will not be Blamed for nothing.'

By this time 600 police and plain-clothes detectives had been deployed in the area, alongside amateur vigilantes, and rumours were rife. The Ripper was a foreign seaman, a Jewish butcher, someone who habitually carried a black bag; and there were attacks on anyone who fitted this description. He could even be – for how else could he so successfully avoid apprehension? – a policeman run mad. There was plenty of time now for speculation. For the Ripper didn't move again for more than a month – and when he did, it was the worst murder of all. His victim was 25-year-old Mary Jane Kelly; and her body, when it was found in the wretched hovel she rented, was unrecognizable: there was blood and pieces of flesh all over the floor. The man who found her later said:

'I shall be haunted by [the sight of it] for the rest of my life.'

This time, though, there was a clue. For Mary Jane had last been seen in the company of a well-dressed man, slim and wearing a moustache. This fitted in with other possible sightings and could be added to the only other evidence the police now had: that the killer was left-handed, probably young – and he might be a doctor for he showed knowledge of human dissection.

After this last murder, though, the trail went completely cold. For the Ripper never killed again. The inquest on Mary Jane Kelly was summarily closed and investigations were called off, suggesting to some that Scotland Yard had come into possession of some very special information, never disclosed. This has left the problem of the Ripper's identity wide open to every sort of speculation. The finger has been variously pointed – among many others – at a homicidal Russian doctor, a woman-hating Polish tradesman, the painter Walter Sickert, the Queen's surgeon and even her grandson, Prince Albert, the Duke of Clarence. The theory in this last case is that Albert had an illegitimate child by a Roman Catholic shopgirl who was also an artist's model. Mary Jane Kelly had acted as midwife at the birth, and she and all the friends she'd gossiped to were forcibly silenced, on the direct orders of the Prime Minister of the day, Lord Salisbury.

The probable truth is that the Ripper was a man called Montague John Druitt, a failed barrister who had both medical connections and a history of insanity in his family. He'd become a teacher, and had subsequently disappeared from his school in Blackheath. A few weeks after the death of Mary Jane Kelly – when the killings stopped – his body was found floating in the river.

THE KRAY TWINS

THE KRAY TWINS, Reggie and Ronnie, were probably the nearest London ever came to producing an indigenous Mafia. On the surface they were legitimate businessmen, the owners of clubs and restaurants haunted by the fashionable rich. But in reality they were racketeers and murderers, protected from prosecution by their reputation for extreme violence.

They were born in the London's East End in 1933 – and soon had a reputation as fighters. Both became professional boxers and, after a brief stint in the army, bouncers at a Covent Garden nightclub. It was then that they started in the protection business, using levels of intimidation that were, to say the least, unusual for their time. Their cousin Ronald Hart later said of them:

> 'I saw beatings that were unnecessary even by underworld standards and witnessed people slashed with a razor just for the hell of it.'

In 1956, Ronnie Kray was imprisoned for his part in a beating and stabbing in a packed East End pub, and judged insane. But three years later he was released from his mental hospital, and the twins were back in business, cutting a secret swath of violence through the British capital while being romanticized in the British press – along with people like actors Michael Caine and Terence Stamp. When they were arrested in 1965 for demanding money with menaces, a member of the British aristocracy actually stood up in the House of Lords and asked why they were being held for so long without trial. They were ultimately acquitted.

In the same year, Ronnie committed his first known murder: of the chief lieutenant of the twins' main rivals for criminal power in London, brothers Eddie and Charles Richardson. George Cornell was shot in the head in another crowded East End pub. But not a single witness was prepared to come forward to testify against Ronnie to police. When Reggie heard the news of what his twin, known as 'the Colonel,' had been up to, he said:

'Well, Ronnie does some funny things.'

Ronnie, though, was exultant at having got away with the killing and having sent out a message that he was above the law.

The Krays with their elder brother Charlie.

'He was very proud...'

said Hart,

'and was constantly getting at Reggie and asking him when he was going to do his murder.'

Two years later Reggie chose his mark, a small-time criminal called Jack 'The Hat' McVitie, who was said to have bad-mouthed the twins. Reggie had McVitie 'escorted' from a Hackney jazz club to a nearby basement, where Reggie stabbed him to death as his brother shouted him on.

In 1969, after a long undercover investigation, the Krays and their henchmen were finally brought to justice, charged with these two murders and with a third: that of an escaped convict called Frank Mitchell, nicknamed the Mad Axe-Man. Though Mitchell's murder was never proved, both twins were given life sentences, with a recommendation that they serve at least 30 years. Their elder brother Charlie, who'd helped to get rid of McVitie's body, was sentenced to ten years.

In 1979, while still in prison, Ronnie was once more declared insane and sent to a mental hospital. But the myth of the Krays as East-End-boys-made-good – men who never forgot a good turn and loved their old neighbourhood and their mother – continued to cling to them. At least two feature films have been made about their lives – in those, too, they resembled the American Mafia. When they died, five years apart, there were massive turn-outs at their East End funerals.

LORD LUCAN

RICHARD JOHN BINGHAM was an arrogant man, a snob. He was a bully-boy, a gambler and risk-taker with an inflated opinion of his own abilities. But he was also Lord Lucan, the seventh earl of that name, and there were all too many parasites around him ready to confirm his sense of his own importance. If he hadn't been Lord Lucan, he might not have committed murder; and if he had, he would have been long forgotten. As it is, almost 30 years after he disappeared, 'Lucky' Lucan sticks in the public memory as a symbol of something rotten in the state of Britain – giving off, for all that, the faintest whiff of glamour.

He may, of course, have simply been mad on the night he killed his children's nanny in November 1974. Certainly he'd been losing heavily at London's gambling-tables; he was now seriously in debt. And certainly he had a pathological hatred of his wife, from whom he'd separated the previous year, losing custody in the process of his children. He'd contended to his cronies that she was insane and at the root of all his current problems. He'd had her watched and followed.

Be that as it may, the facts are these: on the night of 7 November 1974, Lord Lucan's estranged wife Veronica stumbled into a pub opposite her house in London's Belgravia, soaked to the skin, distraught, without shoes and bleeding from a wound in the head. Between sobs, she blurted out an incoherent story about how she'd just escaped from a murderer in her house.

'My children, my children,'

she said;

'he's murdered the nanny.'

The police were immediately called; on entering the house, they found the body of the nanny, Sandra Rivett, battered to death and stuffed into a canvas bag in the basement. 'Lucky' Lucan had apparently let himself into the house, meaning to kill his wife, and had hit out in the dark at the first woman he saw there with a length of lead piping. Then, realizing his mistake, he'd taken her body down to the basement. In the meantime, Veronica Bingham came downstairs to see what had happened to the nanny, and she in turn was attacked.

Her story was that her husband then confessed to killing the nanny by mistake – she was the same height and build as she was. She never explained, however, why this confession seems to have taken all of 40 minutes: the time that elapsed before she ran out for help. Lucan, for his part, had a different story. In a telephone call he made that night to a friend, and then to another friend he later visited outside London, he said that he'd come across an intruder who'd been attacking his wife. Then he completely disappeared.

His passport and the clothes he'd intended to wear that night for a dinner with friends at a gambling club were later found at the house he'd been living in. His car was found near the south coast. No trace of him has ever since been found, though reports that he'd been spotted, in South Africa, Australia, Ireland, the Caribbean and elsewhere, soon began arriving. He is now presumed dead – indeed his son has now succeeded him to the Lucan title. But the rumours – of rich, aristocratic friends who smuggled 'Lucky' Lucan out of the country and still support him – persist.

DENNIS NILSEN

IN FEBRUARY 1983 an engineer was called to a house in north London to investigate a blocked drain. He soon found the cause: backed-up human flesh. The owner of one of the flats in the building – a tall, bespectacled civil servant called Dennis Nilsen – had been flushing the remains of his victims down the lavatory.

But not by any means all of them. For police found in his flat two severed heads and a skull that had been boiled down to the bone, as well as half a male torso and various human parts in the cupboards. They hadn't been kept there for any other reason than Nilsen, living right at the top of the house, had had a problem with disposal. If he hadn't had to move in 1981 from the garden flat he'd previously occupied, where more human bones were later found, he'd probably have gone undetected. For there he'd had options: he'd been able to bury the bones of his dead after crushing their skulls with a garden roller or else burn them on garden fires, with a tyre tossed on top to disguise the smell. At his new address, after dissecting his three victims, he'd had to put out the larger bones for the binmen – and use the lavatory for the rest.

Nilsen, a lonely homosexual, confessed all this more or less immediately, and pointed the police to his previous flat, where they found 13 kilos worth of human bones, all that remained of his 12 earlier victims. The 15 dead had all been homosexuals or drifters whom Nilsen had picked up, brought back to his flat and then strangled while they were asleep or insensible from drink. He didn't, he said, have sex with their corpses or eat their flesh:

'I'm an egg-and-bacon man myself,'

he later said indignantly. His motive seems to have been simply that he wanted company. His first victim had been killed on 30 December 1978, because he'd had a miserable Christmas and wanted someone to share New Year's with him,

'even if it was only a body.'

In October 1983, he was convicted on six charges of murder and two of attempted murder and sentenced to six terms of life imprisonment. During the course of the trial, it became clear that the police had earlier failed to charge him when two separate complaints had been made against him by men he had attacked. They'd also ignored the three carrier-bags full of human flesh found by a microbiologist not far from Nilsen's garden apartment.

Nilsen was sentenced to life imprisonment on 4 November 1983.

WILLIAM PALMER

WILLIAM PALMER, BORN in Rugeley, Staffordshire, in 1825, was only ever tried for a single crime, the death of a racehorse-owner called John Parsons Cook – and for that he was publicly hanged. But there's evidence that he killed at least 15 other people – reason enough for him to be known ever since as The Prince of Poisoners.

Palmer was in his way a throwback, a rake, the sort of man who might have thrived in the Regency period. But he came of age in the much primmer times of Queen Victoria, when middle-class morality ruled. Palmer didn't fit in. Wine, women and gambling were no longer approved of – which is why he became so notorious.

The son of a sawyer – and with a legacy from his dead father which was never quite enough – he seems to have begun stealing at an early age to support the lifestyle he craved. He was sacked for it from his apprenticeship to a Liverpool chemist, and there was more trouble of the same sort when he moved on to study with a surgeon. There was also some suspicion that he was beginning to use his knowledge of toxicology in an inappropriate way. When he was 21, a drinking contest he was having with a man he'd cuckolded came to an abrupt end when his rival suddenly died after just two glasses of brandy.

After qualifying as a doctor in London – and running up debts – he set up a medical practice in his home town and got married to a young woman whose mother was rich and who had an income of her own. But it still wasn't enough to feed his gambling habit, and a number of Palmer's relatives and associates started to die suspiciously. An uncle given to drink died in a drinking bout with him. His mother-in-law passed away ten days after arriving to visit her daughter; and the wife of another uncle fell sick while paying a visit – though she survived after refusing to take the pills he offered as a cure. These were duly followed into the Palmer home by two racing associates to whom he owed money – and who didn't long survive their dinner.

Palmer was able to steer clear of suspicion in this string of murders for three reasons: first, because almost nothing was known outside London at the time about the detection of poisons; second, because he was regarded as a 'gentleman' who would never stoop so low; and third, because he had an elderly doctor in tow, who was only too happy to defer to Palmer's knowledge of medicine. He duly wrote on the death certificates whatever Palmer said: English cholera or apoplexy.

In January 1854, Palmer took out a skein of insurance policies on his wife's life and in September, after a terrible run of luck at the track – which included betting heavily on a horse of his own – he with some reluctance killed her. The following year, he did the same with his brother's life, though this time the insurance companies refused to pay up after he was dead – and said that if he chose to take the case to court, they'd have him investigated for murder.

With his creditors now roaring at his back, he tried the same trick one last time, and killed fellow rake John Parsons Cook after he'd had a big win on a horse of his at Shrewsbury Races. Palmer stole his betting slips and cashed them in; he forged a cheque in his name and he also had the cheek to make a £4,000 claim on his estate. Cook's stepfather became suspicious and had some of the dead man's organs sent to London for analysis. The coroner subsequently recorded a verdict of wilful murder.

By this time Palmer had been arrested for debt on a charge brought by one of his creditors. Now he was sent to Stafford Prison to await the exhumation of his wife's and brother's corpses. The whole of England was abuzz with news of his crimes; and a special Act of Parliament was passed to have him brought to London for trial. The courtroom there was packed and thousands of copies of the transcripts were sold, most of it full of the medical jargon of conflicting experts. For though it was by now known that Palmer had bought strychnine at the time of Cook's death, no trace of it was ever found in his body. The experts gave different reasons for this – and Palmer wouldn't help. All he ever said on the subject was:

'I am innocent of poisoning Cook by strychnine.'

It didn't matter. He was sentenced to death and hanged in front of Stafford Jail on 14 June 1856, with an audience of almost 30,000 people, some in expensive reserved seats. By that time it had been remembered that all of Palmer's children but one had died young of convulsions – and so had at least two of his bastards.

MICHAEL RYAN

IN 1987, MICHAEL Ryan was 27 years old – and a patchily employed farm labourer in Hungerford, west of London. He was ill-educated, morose. His only real passion in life was for guns. He was a member of the local rifle and pistol club where he'd show off his marksmanship and boast to anyone who would listen about his collection of guns – which he kept, fully licensed, in the house he shared with his mother.

No one knows what tipped Michael Ryan over the edge – the best that anyone can come up with is that he was still deeply depressed about the death of his father two years before. But on 19 August 1987, dressed in a military flak jacket and carrying a belt of ammunition, he drove to a nearby forest and, using a 9-mm pistol, shot dead a young woman who was picnicking there with her two children. Then he drove back home, shot both his mother and the family dog and set the house on fire. Picking up his AK-47 from the shed outside, he set out on a leisurely walk through Hungerford.

Who they were didn't matter. He simply killed whoever he saw: a woman and her daughter driving past; a dog-walker; an elderly man working in his garden; another man on his way to the hospital to see his newborn child. In just ten minutes, Michael Ryan calmly killed 16 people and wounded another 14.

The police put up roadblocks and brought in a helicopter and Ryan ultimately took refuge, in a strange sort of symbolism, in the school he himself had gone to as a kid. The police tried to talk him out, but for hours he kept them at bay, saying nothing. Then, seven hours after his first murder, he used his gun on himself: he committed suicide.

The Prime Minister, Margaret Thatcher, said famously about what Ryan had done:

'Dawn came like any other dawn, and by evening it just didn't seem the same day.'

Amid much hand-wringing, Parliament rushed through tougher legislation governing gun-ownership and rifle and pistol clubs – on the grounds that Michael Ryan had used his guns to kill simply because he owned and practised with them. No one, though, has ever satisfactorily explained what was going through his mind – or why he chose that particular day.

JACK SHEPPARD

AS A HIGHWAYMAN, Jack Sheppard, who was hanged in 1724, was by no means major-league – he seems to have spent just one week at it, and to have carried out only three robberies: of a stage-coach, a lady's maid and a grocer. He was caught easily enough. But by the time he had escaped four times – once each from St Giles Roundhouse and the New Prison in Clerkenwell, and twice from the Condemned Hold in Newgate – this young brown-eyed thief with an attractive stammer had become the most celebrated criminal in all 18th-century Britain.

His adventures were published in pamphlets and broadsheets, as well as in column after column in the newspapers. His portrait was painted by Sir James Thornhill, the most fashionable artist of his day. Daniel Defoe took down from him an account of his life; he inspired a series of pictures by William Hogarth; and when he was finally caught for good, people from both town and country – aristocrats and farmers alike – flocked to Newgate to stare at him as he sat chained and manacled to the floor. There are in London, a journalist wrote in 1724:

'three great Curiosities. . . viz: the two young Lyons stuff'd at the Tower; the ostrich on Ludgate Hill; and the famous John Sheppard in Newgate.'

In the week before he was hanged, newspaper coverage went up – one journalist wrote: 'Nothing more at present is talked about Town, than Jack Sheppard.' The king was even said to have asked for:

> 'two prints of Sheppard showing the manner of him being chained... in the Castle in Newgate.'

Such was the publicity that fully 200,000 people turned out to line the processional route he took to the gallows, and after he'd been cut down by the hangman, there were fights over who should have his body. The gang of admirers who finally won it brought him to a City tavern that night, and there was a riot outside that had to be put down by a company of armed Foot Guards.

Within a fortnight, the first of scores of dramatizations of his career opened at Drury Lane; and for the next century and more, fictional versions of his exploits were served up again and again to each successive generation. In 1839, Harrison Ainsworth started publishing his *Jack Sheppard*, which outsold Dickens' *Oliver Twist*. The following year there were no fewer than nine theatrical productions. Well into the 20th century Jack Sheppard remained alive, wept over by children for his difficult life and cruel fate.

DR HAROLD SHIPMAN

HAROLD SHIPMAN IS almost certainly the most prolific serial killer in British history. A public enquiry in 2002 reported that over his career he had probably killed 215 people, mostly women, all of whom had been his patients. For Shipman was a doctor who killed, apparently, simply because he could. His victims were mostly elderly or infirm – they would die sometime, so why not when he dictated? He was caring, after all: a trouble-taker, a pillar of the community always ready to go out of his way to help. So why on earth would anyone suspect him of using the home visits he made to inject his victims with enough heroin or morphine to stop them breathing? No one ever thought to doubt his word and covering his tracks was simplicity itself: all he had to do was doctor his victims' medical records, if that was necessary, and write a fake cause of death, as their personal GP, on the death certificate. There was no need at all, he'd announce, for a post-mortem.

Occasionally Dr Shipman would be mentioned in his patients' wills, of course, but that seemed only natural. They mostly didn't have a great deal of money in the first place; sometimes they had no living family and the doctor, who always worked alone at his surgery in Hyde, Greater Manchester, was the personification of kindness. Then, though, in 1998, he got greedy. For one of his patients, Kathleen Grundy, a woman in her 80s, left him over £380,000. Questions were asked, and the will turned out to have been forged by none other than Shipman himself. He was sentenced to four years in prison.

It was this that triggered a full-scale enquiry. For unlike a great many of his patients – who'd been cremated, along with the evidence in their bones and blood – Kathleen Grundy had been buried. So her body was disinterred and it was found to contain enough heroin to have killed her. Shipman's records were then seized and searched; relatives of dead patients were interviewed and police began the grisly business of recovering and testing as many corpses as they could locate. The list of those murdered via injections began to rise; and so, to the horror of relatives, friends and patients alike, did the roster of probables.

Shipman, who turned out to have a history of drug addiction, was tried on 15 counts of murder, all of which he denied; and in January 2000, he was sentenced to life on each count, with the judge adding that, in his case,

'life would mean life.'

When the subsequent enquiry reported that he had probably been guilty of another 199 murders, he had nothing to say except, again, that he was innocent; at the beginning of 2003, he launched an appeal against his sentence, on the grounds that his legal team hadn't been allowed to conduct their own post-mortems and that the jury had been wrongly instructed. It seems oddly apt that one of the solicitors involved in his appeal also acted for Slobodan Milošević.

On 13 January 2004, the eve of his 58th birthday, Shipman was found hanged in his prison cell.

GEORGE JOSEPH SMITH

WHEN GEORGE JOSEPH Smith, the 'Brides in the Bath' killer, was put on trial at London's Old Bailey in June 1915, a surprising number of women showed up to fill the public seats. But then his small eyes were mesmerizing:

'They were little eyes that seemed to rob you of your will,'

in the words of one of his victims.

Smith was born in the East End of London in 1872 and from the beginning he was a bad lot. At the age of nine, he was sentenced to a reform school for eight years; and by the time he came out, he'd learned all the tricks of the thieving trade. At first he did the thieving himself, but then he discovered his power over women. With a succession of lovers, one of whom he married, he became a small-time Fagin, setting up the robberies they committed and fencing the proceeds.

Ultimately, though, this gambit proved unreliable. For his wife, whom he'd abandoned after she'd been caught and jailed, recognized him one day in a London street, and told the police. He served two years in jail; and when he came out, he turned to a new line of work: using a variety of aliases, he went on an extended tour of the south coast of England, serially seducing women into marriage with him, and then cleaning them out of everything they owned – their savings, their stocks, even their furniture – before he disappeared to start again.

One of these women was 33-year-old Bessie Mundy, a modest heiress whom he 'married' in August 1910 and then unceremoniously abandoned, after failing to get his hands on her whole estate. Eighteen months later, completely by chance, she recognized him on the seafront in Weston-super-Mare while staying with a friend and – incredibly – fell for him yet again. They set up house together and this time Smith found a way to get her money. For five days after they'd both signed wills leaving everything they had to each other, Bessie was found 'drowned' in the bath. A doctor was called, and then the police – but there seemed no reason to suspect the distraught husband's story: that he'd gone out to buy some fish and had returned from his expedition to find his wife dead.

Having now got Bessie's money in its entirety, Smith invested in property in Bristol, where he regularly lived with another of his 'wives', pretending to be in the antiques business – and therefore regularly having to travel. By October 1913, though, he needed a fresh injection of cash. So he 'married' again, this time a private nurse of 25 with money of her own, and took out an insurance policy on her life. After setting up home together, in December of that year they went on holiday to Blackpool and rented a room in a boarding house.

In Blackpool, Smith followed more or less exactly the same pattern as in the first murder. First he called in a doctor to consult about his wife's 'fits'; then a day later, in the evening, he asked the landlady to run a bath. He then went out 'to buy eggs for breakfast,' and returned to find his wife drowned. The doctor was called back to the house, but neither he nor the police nor the coroner at the inquest the next day had any cause to be suspicious. Only the landlady did, for she'd watched what she'd seen as Smith's callous behaviour. When he left immediately after the funeral – to get rid of his wife's belongings as quickly as he could – she shouted 'Dr Crippen' at his back. On the guest card he'd filled in, she wrote presciently:

'Wife died in bath. We shall see him again.'

In December the following year, Smith 'married' once more. But this time he was in a hurry – and it proved his undoing. For on the 17th, he 'married' a clergyman's daughter whom he'd already persuaded to take out life insurance and the next day in London – having speedily got her to make a will and see a doctor about her fits – he killed her. There was no problem with the landlady – 'Mr Lloyd' had returned to the house with a bag of tomatoes before going upstairs – and there was no problem with the coroner, who recorded a verdict of death by misadventure a few days after Christmas. The problem this time was the popular press, for whom this was a story too good to miss. 'Found Dead In Bath,' ran the headline in the *News of the World*: 'Bride's Tragic Fate On Day After Wedding!' The story was read both by the landlady in Blackpool and by the father of one of his two dead 'wives'. It was a coincidence too far.

Smith was arrested in February 1915 and, since he could be only be tried under British law for one murder at a time, proceedings began with the death of Bessie Mundy. Evidence from the other two cases, however, was soon permitted and he didn't help his case by hectoring witnesses, even the judge. The jury in the end took just 22 minutes to find George Smith guilty. He was hanged on 13 August 1915 at Maidstone Prison, mourned only by Bristol 'wife' Edith Pegler: the only one of them all he'd never stolen from, exploited or murdered.

PETER SUTCLIFFE

PETER SUTCLIFFE, THE Yorkshire Ripper, was a hen-pecked husband who had difficulty in getting or maintaining an erection. He only had sex with one of his 13 female victims, and on the night he was caught – 2 January 1981 – he was again having difficulties with a prostitute called Ava Reivers, who would have become his fourteenth. Impotence, in fact, may have driven him to murder in the first place; and killing may have been his sinister way of finding its solution and cure. For at some time in the late-1960s, he'd been publicly humiliated by a prostitute for his inadequacy. So he took his revenge: he began to rape them, not with his penis, but with a knife, a hammer, a sharpened screwdriver – any tool that came to hand.

The first mutilated body was found on playing fields in Leeds on 30 October 1975; the second, less than three months later, in an alleyway nearby. Thirteen months after that a third victim was discovered, stabbed to death, in the same general area, though this time in a suburban park. Though the police took action in all three cases – and the name 'Yorkshire Ripper' was coined in a national newspaper – the respectable folk of the city were not particularly concerned. For all three women, however brutally murdered, had been streetwalkers, sinners, and the killings had been centred on the red-light district of Chapeltown.

With the next two killings, though, the respectable folk of all Yorkshire learned to change their minds. For the Ripper now let it be known that he moved around and might attack any woman at all. On 24 April 1977, he killed a fourth prostitute in another Yorkshire city, in Bradford; and then, back in Leeds again, an ordinary 16-year-old who was involved in nothing more sinister than walking home after an evening out dancing.

With this fifth murder, especially, the people of Yorkshire, indeed of the whole country, began to wake up. The police were inundated with telephone calls, tips, information, supposition – and began to sink under the burden. By this time they had only two pieces of information that firmly linked the murders together: the savagery of the killer's attacks and identical shoeprints that had been found near the bodies of two of the victims. But then, when with the next two attacks really important clues were offered, they clearly failed to see them.

The first, again in Bradford, was on another prostitute who, this time, was savagely beaten but not killed, as if the Ripper had been interrupted.

When she recovered from surgery, she told police that her attacker had been blond and had driven a white Ford Cortina. The second was much further afield, in Manchester; and the victim, again a prostitute, had actually been attacked and mutilated twice, the second time eight days after her death. The police, who found her body a day after the second attack, also found her handbag nearby; and in it was a brand-new £5 note, which turned out to have been issued by a bank in Shipley, Yorkshire. It had formed part of the payroll at the engineering and haulage works where Peter Sutcliffe worked as a truck-driver.

The friendly, unassuming Sutcliffe was interviewed – he was actually interviewed eight times in all during the enquiry. But, though he drove a Ford Cortina, he was not blond, so he was on this occasion eliminated. Apparently the police didn't pay much attention to the handwritten placard this neatly-dressed, diffident man had put up in the cab of his truck:

'In this truck is a man whose latent genius, if unleashed, would rock the nation, whose dynamic energy would overpower those around him. Better let him sleep.'

Sutcliffe seems to have been unfazed by this, his first brush with the law. In short order after this, he battered and mutilated three more prostitutes, in Bradford, Huddersfield and again Manchester; he then killed a 19-year-old building-society clerk as she took a short cut through a park in Halifax. Whatever suspicions the police might have had of him were, in any case, soon dismissed. For the investigating squad at this point received an audio-tape with a taunting message from 'the Ripper', which seemed to contain inside information about the crimes. But the accent 'the Ripper' spoke in wasn't from Yorkshire, as Sutcliffe's was. It was Geordie, said phoneticists – i.e. from the area around Newcastle.

The whole investigation, then, went off at a highly-publicized tangent, and Sutcliffe was free to strike again. In September 1978, he killed a 19-year-old university student in the centre of Bradford and the following August, a respectable 47-year-old civil servant on her way home from the Department of Education in Pudsey. He went on to attack, first a doctor in Leeds and then a 16-year-old girl in Huddersfield – though both survived, the first because he seems to have changed his mind and stopped, and the second because her screams brought people running and scared him away. His final onslaught came more than a year later when a 20-year-old student at Leeds

University got off a bus in a middle-class suburb and started walking towards her hall of residence. Sutcliffe got out of his car and beat her about the head with a hammer, before dragging her across the road into some bushes. He undressed her and stabbed her repeatedly, once straight through the eye, with a sharpened screwdriver because,

'she seemed to be staring at me,'

he said later.

He was finally picked up in Sheffield on 2 January 1981, while sitting in his car with Ava Reivers in a well-known trysting-place for prostitutes and their johns. Police stopped by for a routine check, and wondered why Reivers' client's car seemed to have false number plates. Sutcliffe did his best to get rid of the weapons in the back of the car, but both he and Reivers were taken back to a police station and the weapons were later recovered. After a while, the man who'd given his name as Peter Williams confessed to being the Yorkshire Ripper.

There's been endless speculation about what drove Peter Sutcliffe to murder. Was it because of his worship of his mother and his shyness with girls as a boy? Or because of the time he spent as a young man working first in a graveyard and then in a morgue? Or was it because of the prostitute who'd mocked him in public or the wife who continually nagged him? Was the whole killing spree triggered by his discovery in 1972 that his adored mother was only too human after all – and had long been having a love affair? Whatever the trigger, though, Peter Sutcliffe was found guilty of 13 murders and seven attempted murders. He was sentenced to life imprisonment on each count, with the recommendation that he not be released for at least 30 years. The man with the Geordie accent who sent the police the hoax audiotape – and caused indirectly the deaths of three women – was finally identified, in 2005, as one John Humble and subsequently sentenced to eight years.

DICK TURPIN

LIKE THE HERO-VILLAINS of the Wild West and of the Australian bush, the highwayman Dick Turpin, still familiar until a few years ago to every British schoolboy, belongs as much to folk-myth as to history.

The real Dick Turpin was born in Essex in 1705, the son of a farmer, and was given enough education for him to be able, much later, to pass himself off as a gentleman. Apprenticed to a butcher, by the age of 21 he had his own shop, which he stocked with sheep and oxen stolen from his neighbours. He was spotted, unfortunately, during one of his raids. So he took to the road; became briefly a smuggler and then joined the famous Essex Gang, which specialized in breaking and entering.

The exploits of the members of the Essex Gang were widely written up in the London newspapers at the time. They were violent, knowledgeable about valuables and not above the occasional rape or two in the line of duty. A large reward was put on their heads, and two of them were arrested and hanged in chains. Turpin, who'd only escaped by jumping out of a window, went on the run, hooked up with another highwayman, and began a notorious career robbing travellers and coaches on the roads in and out of London.

Bounty-hunters went after him to no avail. He even appeared from time to time in the City of London. Then, by accident, he shot his partner in a scuffle with a constable and though he continued his hold-up career on his own for a while, he decided, when the bounty on his head doubled, to quit the south of England and ride northward.

In Welton in Yorkshire – though he was widely accepted as a gentleman – he still made a living stealing horses and some of his old habits proved ingrained. One day he blithely shot a cock belonging to his landlord; when one of those present complained, he said if the man would just stand still while he loaded his pistol, he would take pleasure in shooting him too.

A complaint was made. Turpin was arrested and imprisoned in York Castle where his true identity was discovered. He was condemned to death. And it was then that the legend of Turpin – the 'gentleman of the road' – was born. For this (in reality) squat, pocked and swarthy man bought new shoes and a suit before his execution. He gave a vast sum of money to five poor men to follow him to the gallows as mourners and bowed to spectators from the cart that took him to the scaffold,

'with an air of the most astonishing indifference and intrepidity.'

Once there, he chatted to his executioner for half an hour before jumping off the ladder, with the noose around his neck, of his own accord.

In death, Turpin was transmuted into the archetypal free man, a rebel-hero riding his great horse Black Bess into a fictional sunset. He became a central figure in Harrison Ainsworth's immensely popular novel *Rookwood*, and every pub between the two cities seemed to have a memento of his record-breaking – and almost mythical – ride between London and York. Still, who cared? As a later biographer of Turpin wrote:

'Fiction is far stronger and greater than truth!'

FRED AND ROSEMARY WEST

ROSE WEST WAS short, bespectacled and plump. She looked harmless; and when she went on trial in Gloucester in October 1995 on ten counts of murder, she maintained that harmless was exactly what she was. Her husband, Fred West, she said, had killed the two children and eight women involved without her knowledge – he had confessed as much and had insisted that she herself had played no part. Yes, he had hanged himself in a prison cell before coming to trial – and that was unfortunate. But she herself was totally innocent.

In the absence of any eye-witnesses to the crimes, this made the evidence of a woman called Janet Leach especially important. For Leach had been Fred West's 'appropriate adult,' a volunteer assigned to accompany him as a companion during his interviews with the police. She'd visited him many times after he'd been arrested, and she told a different story. For Fred West, out of the interview-room, had told her that it was Rose who'd done the killings and that there were other people involved, including Rose's father and not all the killings had taken place at 25 Cromwell Street, with its one-woman brothel and torture chamber. There was also a deserted farmhouse...

At this point in her testimony, Janet Leach broke down. She became ill – a natural reaction, as anyone who has read an account of the Wests' known crimes will well appreciate. For they were monsters, sexual sadists and predators, who picked up lost souls and raped and tortured them, and didn't even stop at their own daughters.

Fred West was born in 1941, into a family of farm-labourers in the Herefordshire village of Much Marcle; Rose 12 years later, in Northam.

Both seem to have been obsessed with sex from an early age. By the time Rose met Fred, when she was 15, she'd had affairs with several older men; had a history of putting out to truckers at a café where she worked and may have had an incestuous relationship with her own father. As for 27-year-old Fred, he'd been arrested for having sex with a 13-year-old girl; had a

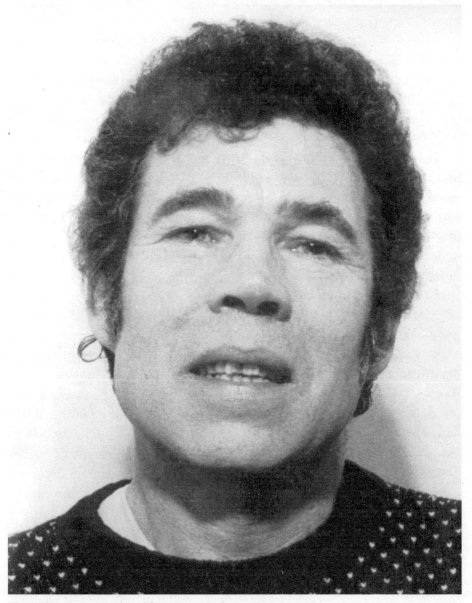

Fred West hanged himself in prison before going to trial.

history of rape and assault and had already killed a girlfriend who'd made a nuisance of herself by becoming pregnant.

They soon began to live together, first in a caravan with Fred's daughter and step-daughter, and then, after Rose got pregnant, in a Gloucester flat. Daughter Heather was born in 1970 – but three kids soon proved too much. So they murdered the step-daughter, and when her mother came looking for her, she was last seen getting into Fred's car...

By this time they were both heavily into pornography, bondage and sado-masochistic sex. Fred acted as Rose's pimp, then watched, photographed and filmed her with her clients. In 1972, when Rose became pregnant again, this time with daughter Mae, they got married and moved to larger premises in Gloucester, at 25 Cromwell Street. It was here that the deadly sex-games reached a new pitch of intensity and the killings began in earnest.

They could have been stopped. If the social services, for example, had ever bothered to examine why eight-year-old Heather had been kept from school, they might have found out that she'd been held down by her mother while her father raped her. If the court had listened properly to the evidence of a 17-year-old, who'd been assaulted, tied up and raped by the pair of them, then it might have done more than fine them £50. And if a mother calling at number 25 in search of her missing daughter – only to be told by Rose that she'd moved away – had gone on to ask Rose why on earth, then, was she wearing the daughter's slippers, she could perhaps have brought an end to the couple's murderous activities.

As it was, over the next 20 years – as Fred constantly expanded and 'improved' the house and garden, and Rose had five more children, two of them by West Indians – they used their older daughters as sex slaves and had regular sex sessions with any woman they could find, willing or unwilling. Some were lodgers, some were drifters and hitchhikers – and those who didn't like it were simply killed after prolonged torture. Daughter Heather was killed because she wanted to leave home and Anna Marie only made it away from the house because she was pregnant with her father's child. It turned out to be an ectopic pregnancy, and she was ultimately aborted.

In 1992, however, the net began to close in. A schoolgirl told a friend of hers that she'd been raped by Fred with the help of Rose, and the friend went to the police. They were arrested, and though the trial collapsed when the schoolgirl refused to give evidence, the police by then had recovered huge quantities of pornographic material from Number 25. They'd also interviewed Anna Marie, who'd told them about her rape and her years of sexual abuse, and they'd heard about the disappearance of Heather, who was rumoured to have been buried under the patio.

After months of persistence by a woman detective called Helen Savage, a police digging-team moved in.

It found nine bodies in all, buried under paving-stones in the garden, and under the cement floors of the cellar and the kitchen extension. Some bore evidence of torture. Fred, then Rose, were arrested; and based on

Rose West claimed her husband had committed the murders.

information Fred gave, police later found the bodies of his first wife, her daughter and the girlfriend Fred had killed before he met Rose. The two women had been buried in fields near Fred's home village of Much Marcle; Charmaine, in the back garden of Fred and Rose's previous flat.

When her case came to trial after Fred had hanged himself, Rose West was found guilty on ten charges of murder and sentenced to life imprisonment. But Janet Leach's testimony still reverberates. For she claimed that Fred had told her: 'The police don't know the half of it.'

And what about the 'deserted farmhouse' he mentioned? The murders Rose was charged with came in three distinct periods: 1973–75, 1978–79 and then a long gap till Heather's death in 1987. It seems unlikely – from such precedents as there are – that the mass murders simply stopped. It seems unlikely too that there weren't accomplices. Perhaps some day the full story of Fred and Rose West will be uncovered.

STEPHEN GRIFFITHS

A PSYCHOLOGY GRADUATE and PhD student in Applied Criminal Justice Studies, Stephen Griffiths is destined to be remembered as 'The Crossbow Cannibal'. The gruesome moniker didn't come from the popular press, but from the man himself. On 28 May 2010, he stood in a packed magistrates' court and boldly gave the name in place of his own. The declaration was met with gasps from a crowd that had no idea what it was he had done with the three women he was accused of murdering.

Stephen Shaun Griffiths was born in Dewsbury, West Yorkshire, on 24 December 1969. A neighbour recalls that as a child the boy liked killing and dismembering birds: 'It looked as if he was enjoying what he was doing. He wasn't dissecting them bit by bit, he was ripping them apart.'

When Griffiths was still very young, his parents split up. He moved with his mother, sister and brother to the nearby city of Wakefield. There he attended the exclusive Queen Elizabeth Grammar School, the alma mater of serial killer John George Haigh, 'The Acid Bath Murderer'.

Griffiths was often in trouble with the law. At the age of 17, he slashed a supermarket manager with a knife when he was stopped for shoplifting. Griffiths received a three-year sentence for that attack, some of which was spent at a high-security mental hospital.

Griffiths managed to earn a degree in psychology from Leeds University. He was accepted at the University of Bradford, where he began work on an academic thesis, 'Homicide in an Industrial City', comparing modern murder techniques in Bradford to those of the 19th century. Griffiths incorporated some of his research in 'The Skeleton and the Jaguar', a website he established that focused largely on serial killers.

Griffiths was arrested numerous times for domestic violence. In 2008, local librarians reported him for borrowing books on human dismemberment. However, it's more than likely that the true number of women murdered by Stephen Griffiths will never be known. Ultimately, he would admit to just three, the first being 43-year-old sex worker and heroin addict Susan Rushworth.

On 26 April 2010, another prostitute, 31-year-old Shelley Armitage, disappeared from downtown Bradford. Two days passed before she was reported missing.

Less than a month later, on 21 May, a Friday, Suzanne Blamires also vanished. Blamires accompanied Griffiths to his flat, most likely willingly, but then she tried to leave. Security cameras captured her sudden end. Grainy footage shows Blamires fleeing Griffiths' flat with the PhD student in pursuit. He knocks her unconscious, and leaves her lying in the corridor. Moments later, he returns with a crossbow, aims and shoots a bolt through her head. Before dragging the woman back into his apartment, he raises his crossbow to the camera in triumph. Moments later, Griffiths returns with a drink, apparently toasting the death.

The first person to view these images was the building caretaker. He called the police – but not before first selling the story to a tabloid newspaper.

The first body was discovered by a member of the public in the River Aire. The corpse was cut into at least 81 separate pieces. Police recovered a black suitcase containing the instruments Griffiths had used to carry out the dissection prior to consuming several pounds of flesh. Identification came without the need for DNA testing – Blamires' head, complete with crossbow bolt, was found in a rucksack. At some point Griffiths had also embedded a knife in her skull.

Griffiths gradually opened up about the murders, providing police with macabre details. He described his flat's bathtub as a 'slaughterhouse', saying that it was there that his victims were dismembered. He used power tools on the first two bodies, boiling the parts he ate in a pot. Blamires was cut up by hand, and her flesh was eaten raw.

Griffiths had filmed his second victim's death on his mobile phone, which he then left on a train. The device was bought and sold twice before police managed to track it down. The footage it held was described by one veteran detective as the most disturbing he'd ever viewed. Armitage is shown naked and bound with the words 'My Sex Slave' spray-painted in black on her back. Griffiths can be heard saying: 'I am Ven Pariah, I am the Bloodbath Artist. Here's a model who is assisting me.'

Only Susan Rushworth was spared the indignity of having her death caught on camera. Investigators believe that she was killed with a hammer.

On 21 December 2010, three days before his 41st birthday, Griffiths pleaded guilty to all three murders and was given a life sentence.

AUSTRALIA

JACK DONOHOE

THE IRISH BUSHRANGER Jack Donohoe was probably 24 years old in 1830, when he was killed by police and a volunteer posse at Bringelly, near Campbelltown outside Sydney. But his memory still endures, kept alive through a popular ballad with hundreds of different variants which lasts down to this day. He became through the ballad the symbol of resistance both to the old convict system and to the British colonial yoke. He is, if you like, both the Jesse James of Australia and, via the heady distillation of the ballad's lyrics, the first standard-bearer of Australian independence.

Sentenced to transportation in Dublin in 1823 at the age of 17, 'Bold' Jack Donohoe was a short, blond, freckle-faced man who, after he arrived in Sydney, seems to have found nothing much but trouble. Having survived the long sea-voyage, he was handed over to a settler in Parramatta, but soon misbehaved: he was sentenced to a stint in a punishment gang to teach him a lesson. Having survived this, he was reassigned, but he took off instead into the bush. In the words of the ballad:

'He'd scarcely served twelve months in chains upon the Australian
    shore,
When he took to the highway as he had done before:
He went with Jacky Underwood, and Webber and Walmsley too,
These were the true companions of bold Jack Donohoe.'

Donohoe's gang, to stay alive, held up the carts that travelled, carrying produce to and from the Sydney settlement, along the Windsor Road. He and two of his henchmen were soon caught and condemned to death. The other two were hanged. But Donohoe, while being returned from court to the condemned cell, made a run for it – further contributing to his reputation:

'As Donohoe made his escape, to the bush he went straightway.
The people they were all afraid to travel by night or day,
For every day in the newspapers they brought out something new,
Concerning that bold bushranger they called Jack Donohoe.'

After stealing horses from settlers, a new Donohoe gang began to roam through a huge swath of territory, holding up travellers, thieving from farms and selling off whatever booty they got to whoever would have it. Back in Sydney, he became a stick with which the newspapers could beat the despised Governor's head. He had armed soldiers and mounted cavalry, they said,

> 'but the bushranging gentry seem to carry on their pranks without molestation.'

They even began to lionize Donohoe himself, whom they praised not only for his dress and sense of style, but also for his Pimpernel quality.

'Donohoe, the notorious bushranger,' announced the *Australian*,

> '...is said to have been seen by a party well acquainted with his person, in Sydney, enjoying, not more than a couple of days ago... a ginger-beer bottle.'

The Governor was finally forced to act. The price on Donohoe's head was raised and more police and volunteers were sent into the field. Finally, at Bringelly, they caught up with him:

> 'As he and his companions rode out one afternoon,
> Not thinking that the pangs of death would overtake them soon,
> To their surprise the Horse-Police rode smartly into view,
> And in double-quick time they did advance to take Jack Donohoe.'

Before it was all over, according to the ballad, Donohoe shouted out his defiance, saying that he'd never be an Englishman's slave. He killed nine men with nine bullets before being shot himself through the heart and asking, with his dying breath, all convicts to pray for him. The truth is, of course, more mundane. He did not kill nine men; he screamed nothing much but obscenities; and he was shot in the head by a trooper called Muggleston. But it didn't matter. For 'Bold' Jack Donohoe was already passing into legend. When his body was laid out in the Sydney morgue, the Colony's distinguished Surveyor-General came in to draw his portrait; and a Sydney shopkeeper produced a line of clay pipes, featuring his head with a bullet-hole at the temple. They sold out fast.

NED KELLY

NED KELLY, A quiet, soft-spoken man, it's said, was the last and greatest of Australia's folk-hero bushrangers, with a fanatical hatred of the law. His father, a Victoria farmer, had been transported as a convict from Belfast in Ireland in 1841, and he himself had spent three years in prison as a boy for horse- and cattle-stealing. Whatever the source of the hatred, though, it seems to have boiled over when a police constable arrived at the Kelly farmstead one day in April 1878, looking for his brother Dan. The whole family resisted; the constable was wounded and when a warrant was issued for Ned and Dan Kelly, they took to the bush with two other young tearaways, Steve Hart and Joe Byrne.

In October of that year, they fought a gun battle with a police patrol sent after them at Stringybark Creek. A sergeant and two troopers were killed and from that moment on Ned Kelly, aged just 23, became Australia's Public Enemy Number One. Identifying him was one thing, though; catching him quite another. For not only did Kelly and his gang have an old and intimate knowledge of the Victoria countryside, they also had many sympathizers – particularly, it's said, among women – who put them up and passed on information about the police's whereabouts. When the Kelly gang robbed its first bank at Euroa in December of that year – after taking 20 hostages – the police were 100 miles away on a wild goose chase.

In February 1879, in any case, the gang left Victoria for New South Wales and robbed a bank in Jerilderie, with 30 local people locked up in a hotel as insurance. Kelly's reputation as a brazen and defiant criminal spread, and the police became a laughing-stock as he continued to evade capture, despite the arrest of some of his sympathizers and the posting of large rewards. Finally, in June 1880, Kelly decided to humiliate them still further. He sent Joe Byrne to Beechworth, where Byrne calmly shot a former accomplice of the gang, who was supposed to be under police protection. Then he took off, aiming to draw a large body of police into a train ambush at Glenrowan, where Kelly had already taken over 60 hostages and had had a section of the track removed.

Warned by a local schoolmaster, though, the police stopped the train and turned the tables: 37 strong, they ambushed the gang, who were holed up in a hotel with their hostages. Ned Kelly, wounded, escaped into the bush; in the middle of the seven hour siege, during which all the other members of the gang died, he reappeared with his guns – and entered Australian history for ever – wearing black face- and body-armour made from iron plough mouldboards. He was only brought down by being shot in the legs. The armour had taken 25 bullets. Asked why he'd come back when he could have escaped, Kelly said:

'A man gets tired of being hunted like a dog. . . I wanted to see the thing end.'

He was hanged in Melbourne in front of a huge crowd in November 1880 – his last words were:

'Such is life.'

But not long afterwards his armour was put on show in Hobart, Tasmania, in an ex-convict ship, along with waxworks and mementoes of the convict-transport system. The ship, which was later moved to Sydney, was scuttled there, armour and all, by indignant citizens who didn't want to be reminded of such things.

KATHERINE KNIGHT

KATHERINE KNIGHT HAD a talent for decapitating pigs. The razor sharp boning knives she had used in her working life in the abattoirs of New South Wales would be the very same tools she later employed to kill her common-law husband.

Knight exhibited a terrifying streak of violence in the years leading up to the murder. She would cut up boyfriends' clothes and vandalize their cars in fits of rage. There were reports too of her involvement in strangulation, stabbing, burning and savage beatings. She once placed her first-born, Melissa, on railway tracks minutes before a train was due – because the father had walked out on her, driven away by Katherine's jealousy and violent behaviour. (The two-month-old baby only escaped almost certain death because a local drifter happened to come along at the right time.) A few days later, she disfigured a 16-year-old girl's face with a butcher's knife. Later, she would further practise her slaughter skills on her partner's eight-week-old puppy, cutting its throat in front of her horrified boyfriend.

In 1994, Knight met John Price, known as 'Pricey'. He was a well-liked man; even his former wife, with whom he'd had four children, spoke of him only in glowing terms. The relationship with Katherine was not easy – the couple often had terrible fights – but six years later Kath and Pricey were still together. By early 2000, though, Pricey began to share his concerns about the relationship with friends and colleagues. He even told a local magistrate that he feared for his life, showing him a stab wound he'd received from Kath. The end of their tempestuous union would come on 29 February 2000.

Knight later claimed she had no recollection of what happened that evening. We know from forensic evidence, though, that at some point Knight donned a black negligee bought at a local charity shop. It's probable that she was wearing the flimsy garment when she and Pricey had sex – it is certain that she had it on when she began stabbing him, at least 37 times, destroying nearly all of his major organs.

At 7:45 am the following morning, Pricey's boss phoned the local police to report that his employee had not yet arrived at work. The authorities visited Pricey's bungalow, forced the door and found his skin hanging in a doorway. His decapitated corpse was lying in the living room, and his head was in a large pot, simmering away on the kitchen stove. On the dining room table were two servings of food, consisting of boiled vegetables and generous portions of cooked corpse. Placement cards indicated that the two settings were intended for Pricey's children.

In October 2001, Knight changed her not guilty plea and admitted that she had killed John Price. The following month she became the first woman in Australia to receive a life sentence without the possibility of parole. Speculation remains as to whether she ate any of the meal prepared from Pricey's body.

WILLIAM MACDONALD

THERE WAS A sigh of relief in Australia in the 1960s when the identity of a homosexual serial killer known as The Mutilator was finally established. For he turned out to be William Macdonald, an Englishman, who claimed in his defence that he'd been raped at the age of 15 by a British army corporal. All this had happened in England, thousands of miles away from the home of proper men. He was not, after all, home-grown.

The search for The Mutilator began in July 1961, when the body of a 41-year-old blacksmith was found under a shed beside the Domain Baths in Sydney. The corpse had been stabbed 30 times; the genitals hacked off, and an attempt had been made to sever the head.

The sheer frenzy of the attack suggested to the police that the motive was jealousy, the revenge of some rival lover or husband. But then, five months later, another man's body, mutilated in exactly the same way, was found in a public toilet in a Sydney suburb. Because of its location, the police began to take for granted that the man they were looking for was 'a psychopath homosexual… killing to satisfy some twisted urge.'

It wasn't until four months later, in March 1962, that The Mutilator struck once more. A young couple with a baby found the still-breathing body of an emasculated man lying in a gutter in another Sydney suburb. The killer had not quite finished his work. Frank Maclean had only been stabbed in the neck, but he'd already lost too much blood from his other major wound to be able to talk. He died shortly afterwards.

The government now offered a large reward for information leading to The Mutilator's arrest, but for another seven months there was not a whisper. Then, in November of that year, a deputy inspector of health went to an unoccupied surburban shop where neighbours had been complaining of a bad smell. Under the building at the back was the partly decomposed body of a man who bore all the sadistic marks of The Mutilator.

The corpse, despite some misgivings on the part of the coroner, was identified as that of Alan Edward Brennan, an ex-post-office sorter who recently opened the shop – and had since disappeared. Trouble was that, six months after he'd been buried, a fellow employee met Brennan on Sydney's George Street. A belated examination of the clothes on the corpse showed that they were in fact prison-issue, and had been given to a man called Patrick Hackett, who'd served a short sentence the previous October for indecent language.

The case now fell into place. For a neighbour remembered seeing Brennan with another man in the shop on the night before his disappearance. A notice had appeared at the shop's door the next day, saying that the owner had cut his hand and would be away for three weeks. Upstairs in the bedroom, along with a bloodstained pillow, had been found a copy of a book about Jack the Ripper…

An Identikit picture of Brennan was published in the press; and was recognized by two clerks at the Spencer Street Railroad Station in Melbourne as fitting a station assistant there called David Allan. 'Allan' was arrested and later confessed – not only to the murders, but also to his real name, William Macdonald. He was taken to Sydney and tried for the murder of Patrick Hackett, whom he'd picked up, drunk, he said, outside a Sydney hotel. He was sentenced to life in prison, and later transferred to the Morriset Mental Hospital for the Criminally Insane.

'CHOPPER' READ

MARK BRANDON 'CHOPPER' Read is a career criminal turned celebrity. He has written a series of books about his experiences and the 2000 film *Chopper* was based on his life.

Born in 1954, Read spent his first five years in a children's home. His mother was a Seventh Day Adventist and his father, an ex-army martinet, used to beat him. He was bullied at school. At the age of 14 he was made a ward of state and as a teenager he was placed in several mental institutions.

By his mid-teens he was the leader of the Surrey Road gang. Then he began robbing drug dealers, removing his victims' toes with bolt-cutters or a blowtorch if they were reluctant to give him their money.

When released from jail in the 1980s, he also claimed to have extorted money from fellow criminals by strapping a stick of gelignite to his chest and threatening to blow them both up if they did not pay up. 'I can't believe I ever had the audacity,' said Read later. 'I also can't believe that it always worked.'

Between the ages of 20 and 38, Read spent just 13 months out of jail, serving time for armed robbery, assault and kidnapping. In Pentridge prison's H division, he started a gang war, leading the so-called 'Overcoat Gang', who wore long coats to conceal their weapons.

During his time in Pentridge, he was said to have attacked 63 men and tried to kill 11. He also had his ears cut off, though there are conflicting stories about how this occurred. His stomach was slit open and he lost several feet of his intestine, but he says that he took his revenge – both in jail and outside.

Read always reckoned that the one crime that brought him to public prominence was the 1987 shooting of the drug dealer, Siam 'Sammy the Turk' Ozerkam, outside Bojangles Nightclub in St Kilda, Melbourne. 'I've pulled the shotty out and gone bang and it's bye, bye, Turk,' said Read, though he still maintains it was an act of instinctive self-defence.

While in jail in 1990, Read began writing to John Silvester, a journalist who had written about him in the *Melbourne Age*. He had a talent for telling stories and his letters were edited into book form and published as *Chopper: From the Inside* the following year. A series of 12 more volumes followed, including a children's book. Material from his prison books provide the material for the movie *Chopper*.

In 2001, Read appeared in an award-winning TV drink-drive campaign, saying: 'When I was in prison I got slashed down the face, my ears cut off, I had a claw hammer put through my brain just here, cut-throat razors here and here, butcher's knife there, ice-pick there, ice-pick up the back there... If you drink and drive and you're unfortunate enough to hit somebody, you ought to pray to God that you don't go to prison.' In 2005, he toured Australia with the show 'I'm Innocent with Mark "Jacko" Jackson'. His name was also used to promote beer.

While in jail Read contracted hepatitis C from sharing a razor. In 2008, he refused a liver transplant on the grounds that there were more deserving cases, but he did give up drinking to prolong his life. How much can we believe of what he's told us? 'Once you pick up pen and paper, you can take people on a journey anywhere,' he says 'The trouble is they come back later on and ask: "Is that true?" I say: "Who gives a sh*t?"'

PICTURE CREDITS

Press Association: 52

Public Domain: 35, 46, 85, 133

Topham Picturepoint: 16, 20, 44, 63, 73, 75, 85, 87, 93, 97, 101, 116, 124, 135, 146, 158, 162, 168, 170, 176, 193, 195

Topfoto: 155